Anna Freud in the Hampstead Clinic:

Letters to Humberto Nágera

Anna Freud in the Hampstead Clinic:

Letters to Humberto Nágera

Edited by Daniel Benveniste PhD
Foreword by Humberto Nágera MD

IPBOOKS.net
International Psychoanalytic Books

A. I. P. The American Institute for Psychoanalysis
American Psychodynamic Press Book Series

Copyright © 2015 Daniel S. Benveniste, Ph.D
Published for the American Psychodynamic Book Series
by
International Psychoanalytic Books (IPBooks),
25–79 31st Street Astoria, NY 11102
Online at: http://www.IPBooks.net and by
The American Institute for Psychoanalysis
329 East 62nd Street
New York, NY 10065
aipkh@aol.com

Photos of documents are used by permission of Sigmund Freud Copyrights.

All rights reserved. This book may not be reproduced, transmitted, or stored in whole or in part by any means, including graphic, electronic, or mechanical without the express permission of the publisher and author, except in the case of brief quotations embodied in critical articles and reviews.

ISBN: 0996548114
ISBN: 9780996548113

Dedicated to the life, work, and inspiration of

Miss Anna Freud

Acknowledgements

This collection of letters from Miss Anna Freud to Dr. Humberto Nágera brings into high relief the collaborative nature of their work together. Compiling the letters into this annotated volume was also a collaboration and so I'd like to thank my publisher Dr. Arnold D. Richards at International Psychoanalytic Books and his team: Lawrence L. Schwartz, Tamar Schwartz, Kathy Kovacic, and Phyllis Stern. They are the ones that saw the material as worthy of publication and transformed the manuscript into a book. Frances Marton at the Carter-Jenkins Center, was helpful in getting documents photographed in record time.

Special thanks go to Dr. Humberto Nágera for permission to publish these letters and photographs from his personal collection. These letters and documents of Anna Freud are published by permission of The Marsh Agency Ltd on behalf of The Estate of Anna Freud, and our special thanks go to Charlotte Bruton and the others involved at the Marsh Agency Ltd for kindly granting this permission. Thanks go to Mag. Peter Prokop at the Österreichische Nationalbibliothek Bildarchiv und Grafiksammlung for permission to publish the photo of a young Anna Freud at her desk in Vienna. Thanks also to the following for permission to republish Anna Freud's forewords to books written by Humberto Nágera: Random House, Basic Books, and Jason Aronson.

Table of Contents

Acknowledgements..vii

Foreword..xi

Introduction: Anna Freud and her Collaboration
with Humberto Nágera... 1

Anna Freud's Letters to Humberto Nágera And Related Documents.....21

References..219

Index...227

Foreword

I WENT TO LONDON in 1958 in order to pursue my psychoanalytic training at the Institute of the British Psychoanalytical Society. While there, in a meeting that the candidates had regularly with Dr. Ilse Hellman, she mentioned that she, Anna Freud, and a group of senior analysts were discussing the issue of narcissism. As it happened, I had written a short paper on the subject of Freud's development of the concept of narcissism throughout his lifetime. She asked me whether I could give her a copy, which, of course, I did. Apparently, she took it to Miss Freud, who read it and liked it very much. That led to my being invited to attend many of the functions of the Hampstead Clinic. So that is how I found my way into the Hampstead Clinic, despite the fact that I had been told, before going to London, that it was not easy to become associated with the Clinic, for a variety of different reasons.

A friend of mine, Dr. Gabriel Casuso, had been in London and had tried to become a member of the staff at Hampstead, but it had not been possible. Thus, he warned me that it might be difficult to get onto the staff of the Clinic. In any case, given that I had gone to London with a student visa, and had my own personal resources to finance my training, I did not need a salary at that point, and so I attended many of the functions of the Hampstead Clinic and became very involved in many of the activities there.

It was soon clear that I had become very helpful in a variety of ways to the functioning of the Clinic, the research programs, and so on, and so a close relationship soon developed between Anna Freud and myself.

Shortly thereafter, a disaster took place in my home country of Cuba, when it fell to a communist takeover, which created a very difficult situation for me.

The new government took over (stole) all my financial resources, leaving me in England with nothing but a student visa, with which I was unable to obtain paid employment. That situation was solved after a while, and you will see in these letters how kind and helpful Anna Freud was through all of this.

I was given political asylum in England because of the threats I had received from the Cuban government, and this asylum allowed me to be employed and earn money in England. Anna Freud was very willing to hire me immediately, since I had already proven my potential value to the Clinic. At that point, she didn't want me to leave, and the way she behaved is perhaps a very good example of how helpful she always tried to be, whenever it was possible for her to be of assistance to anybody in need.

After a few years, I had become a very close professional associate of hers. She then discussed with me her wish for me to become the Director of the Hampstead Clinic, taking her position after her death. I felt honored and agreed to her proposal, and indeed planned to do just that. In her plan I would have taken her position as the Director of the Clinic, and Dr. John Bolland would have been the Medical Director. Unfortunately, the events in Cuba developed in such a way that my wish to stay in England and take over the Clinic upon her death became absolutely impossible.

I needed to emigrate to the United States, because I suddenly found myself having to support not only my own family, but my parents and my wife's parents as well, given that all of them were dispossessed of everything that they had earned during their lifetimes. Thus, given their ages, I became their only possible source of support. Given the type of taxation that existed in England at that time, there was no way that I could keep three families in London. Consequently, and regretfully, I had to leave England in May of 1968, and went to the United States, to the University of Michigan.

Miss Freud fully understood what my obligations were. Nevertheless, we continued our correspondence for many years, indeed, until just a few months before her death. Her letters reveal her feelings, her enormous kindness, her longings, her ambitions, her helpfulness, and her devotion to psychoanalysis, to her father, and to the Hampstead Clinic. Her devotion to the children being treated there was enormous: those she treated herself, the families she had

FOREWORD

contact with and helped, the children who were refugees of concentration camps, and so on. All of these efforts were parts of the on-going development of the Hampstead Child-Therapy Clinic, which was her Clinic, and where I became a staff member.

A couple of vignettes may further convey the kind of person that Miss Freud really was. She was incredibly talented and capable, with an enormous ability as a psychoanalyst. She was an excellent lecturer and theoretician, endowed with a special ability to make very clear any difficult theoretical or clinical matters. She had, as well, many other personal qualities that made her the unique and special person that she was. I have two vignettes to share that exemplify what I have in mind.

When I was a member of the staff of the Clinic, I had an office on the first floor, which meant that a lot of people stopped by my office to say hello, and talk about one thing or another, which was very nice, but pretty much interrupted my ability to work. Thus, when an office became available on the fourth floor, I moved up there. Now, Anna Freud frequently had to come to see me and talk to me about one issue or another, and, to show how extremely considerate and respectful she was of other people, she would come and climb up to the fourth floor. She had some respiratory difficulties, so she naturally got there out of breath. I had to ask her to please not do that anymore, but to just call me on the phone, and I would come down to the ground floor. From that time onwards, I went down whenever she came to see me, which was practically daily.

The second vignette, and in relation to the same subject, is that one day when I got to my new fourth floor office, I found there were some new beautiful orange curtains placed on the window. I was surprised by this change, and made some inquiries. I then found out that in fact, Miss Freud, who was an extraordinary weaver and did a lot of weaving (you can see some examples of it on the web page of the Carter-Jenkins Center), had one day met my daughter in the street near the Clinic. My daughter was then nine or ten years old, and Miss Freud asked her if she knew what my favorite color was. My daughter told her it was orange (which was not necessarily the case), and Miss Freud then wove the curtains in orange and installed them herself in the window. That should give you an idea of how kind, concerned, affectionate, and interactive a person she was.

The letters gathered together in this volume describe for you the activities of Miss Freud during these 29 years, and in particular, the 10 years during which I was at the Clinic, and the close relationship that we developed. You can see how these letters make Miss Freud suddenly very present, and reveal her values and interests in a very real and very clear manner. I am eternally grateful for what I learned from her and for this unique opportunity that life gave to me.

Humberto Nágera, M.D.
Tampa, Florida
November 5, 2013

Introduction: Anna Freud and her Collaboration with Humberto Nágera

Daniel S. Benveniste, Ph.D.

Psychoanalysis is a human tradition passed on from one generation to the next. This collection of letters and related documents are a testament to the fertile collaboration between Anna Freud and Humberto Nágera, and through these documents we witness the passing of the torch. Their work together was based at the Hampstead Clinic in London, and included clinical work, theoretical seminars, research, and cooperation in the management of administrative tasks at the Clinic. When Dr. Nágera informed me of this collection of letters, I immediately recognized that they documented one of the most fertile periods in Anna Freud's career, and were, therefore, worthy of inclusion in the literature on psychoanalytic history. I was honored to take on the editorial task, and found Dr. Nágera very helpful in answering my questions about people and places mentioned in the letters. I found, embedded in these letters and documents, keys to understanding the relationship between Anna Freud's personality and her work, which developed in the context of her relationships with others. A history of this kind presents the major contributor to psychoanalysis not as a larger-than-life person, but as a dedicated and gifted analyst working within an historical context and professional environment.

Humberto Nágera was born in Cuba in 1927, and did his undergraduate work at the University of Havana, and his medical studies at Havana Medical School (1952). After becoming a psychiatrist he sought psychoanalytic training, and began as a psychoanalytic candidate at the Institute of the British Psychoanalytical

Society in 1958, and a trainee at the Hampstead Clinic in 1959. Soon after his arrival at the Hampstead Clinic he became a trusted colleague of Anna Freud and collaborated with her as one of her closest associates during one of the most productive periods of her life. He left London and the Clinic in 1968, but maintained his correspondence with her until her death in 1982.

What we learn from these letters and related documents is a bit about Anna Freud's personality: her shyness, her drive to work; her pursuit of knowedge; her collaborative spirit; her disappointments; her commitment to children, and her tireless and unwavering dedication to psychoanalysis. This collection of letters brings into high relief Anna Freud's work in the 1960s and in this way stands as a companion volume to the various biographies and collections of Anna Freud letters that have already been published. These naturally include: Raymond Dyer's *The Work of Anna Freud* (1983), Elizabeth Young-Bruehl's *Anna Freud: A Biography* (1988), Rose Edgcumbe's *Anna Freud: A View of Development, Disturbance and Therapeutic Techniques* (2000), Peter Heller's book *Anna Freud's Letters to Eva Rosenfeld* (1992), covering the period from 1927 to 1932, Ingeborg Meyer-Palmedo's *The Sigmund Freud, Anna Freud Correspondence 1904–1938* (2013), and my own work, *The Interwoven Lives of Sigmund, Anna and W. Ernest Freud: Three Generations of Psychoanalysis* (2015).

Biographical and historical works about psychoanalysts and psychoanalysis are often pulled in the direction of idealization or denigration: the brilliant self-made hero or the rogue. Taking a middle path, and a particularly psychological one, is to recognize the personal and historical contexts of the major contributor to psychoanalysis, and in doing so, become inspired by their work in order to carry on with our own.

When we examine the personal and historical contexts of the major contributors to psychoanalysis, we discover, not surprisingly, that they were thoroughly embedded in their times and had lives thoroughly interwoven with those around them. Who would Anna Freud have been without the

INTRODUCTION: ANNA FREUD AND HUMBERTO NÁGERA

First and Second World Wars? Who would she have been without her father, Sigmund Freud, without Eva Rosenfeld, Dorothy Burlingham, August Aichhorn, Siegfried Bernfeld, Willi Hoffer, Josephine Stross, Ernest Jones, Marie Bonaparte, Lou Andreas Salome, and an army of students and colleagues throughout the decades? And who would she have been without Melanie Klein as a counterpoint?

There were a number of important colleagues close to Anna Freud in the last productive chapter of her life, but clearly Humberto Nágera was one of the most deeply involved with her work at the Hampstead Clinic, where they managed clinical and administrative tasks together and collaborated closely on the Developmental Profiles and the research and publication of four volumes on the Core Psychoanalytic Concepts. These and other projects contain within them affirmations of Anna Freud's position as a leading ego psychologist.

When we read these letters, we see how quickly Anna Freud becomes impressed with Nágera's intelligence, psychoanalytic sophistication, and his extraordinary capacity for work, which matched hers. Nágera was Anna Freud's student and was 32 years her junior, but they were kindred spirits, and she quickly came to trust him, collaborate with him, and then to rely on him in many matters.

Anna Freud was a particularly talented, productive, and prolific psychoanalyst. She was highly regarded as an analyst, a theoretician, and a creator of institutions dedicated to the care of children. She was famous as a discussant for her dazzling summations of case presentations, and her ability to summarize and historically contextualize a theoretical presentation; and if the presentation was a poor one, she had the ability to find the "speck of gold" within it and highlight that. Furthermore, I think one would be hard pressed to find any analyst in the history of psychoanalysis, living or dead, who has demonstrated more genuine care for children in times of war and hardship than Anna Freud.

When a person obtains a little self-knowledge, he or she knows just that. But when one obtains self-knowledge to great depths, that knowledge extends down into the depths of the human condition. This has been the case over and over again with the great discoveries in the depth psychologies, such as with Freud and the Oedipus complex, Adler and the inferiority complex, Rank and the trauma of birth, Erikson and the identity crisis, Kohut and the Self, and so on. Our deepest interests often contain autobiographical components. Sometimes one can read the professional bibliography of an author and discern persistent themes with an autobiographical basis. So, what might we say about the contributions of Anna Freud and their autobiographical components?

We typically think of Anna Freud as the staunch defender of her father's vision of psychoanalysis. We recall her profound understanding and dedication to his work, her close relationship to her father, and her dedication to his physical care. But on the other side was a highly conflicted relation to her mother. While she identified strongly with her father, she had a weak identification with her mother and the feminine roles that her mother modeled. Consequently, Anna Freud looked to Marie Bonaparte and Lou Andreas Salome as female figures with whom she could more closely identify. Simply put, her relationship with her father was a fairly happy identification, while her most troubling conflicts were with her mother. And to what did she dedicate her life and her research? To the mother-child bond; to child analysis; to the vicissitudes of the maternal bond in institutional care; to disruptions in the maternal relationship; and to the normal and pathological developments of early childhood.

But there was another important psychological dynamic in Anna Freud's life – her relationship to her sister, Sophie. Sigmund and Martha Freud had six children. There was one daughter followed by three boys, and then came Sophie, born in 1893 and Anna, born in 1895. Sophie and Anna, only two years apart, engaged in a bitter sibling rivalry throughout their childhood, adolescence, and into early adulthood. While the two jealously battled for the love and attention of their parents, Anna, as the younger sister, also admired Sophie and wanted to be liked by her. While Anna was more identified with her father, her father was relatively unavailable to her in her early childhood. Sophie, on the other hand, was feminine, pretty, and well-identified with the female roles her mother presented as wife, mother

INTRODUCTION: ANNA FREUD AND HUMBERTO NÁGERA

and homemaker. And of course, their mother, Martha Freud, was far more available to the children in early childhood than their father was (Young-Bruehl, 1988, pp. 23–102).

Entering adolescence and young adulthood, Anna was unable to find love, and instead devoted herself to teaching young children, which in the light of the rest of her history we might see as a kind of foster-mother role. While she may well have yearned for a mother, or foster-mother, with whom she could identify, she turned the tables and altruistically cared for the children of others, first as a teacher, then as an analyst, and later as a nursery and clinic director. From her conflicts in relation to her mother, she developed the role of the child analyst. From her conflicts with her sister Sophie, we see her recurring psychoanalytic interest in the themes of jealousy and altruism. Furthermore, I speculate that in her warm relation to Dorothy Burlingham and in her bitter rivalry with Melanie Klein, we see the two aspects of her early relation to her sister, Sophie.

With this in mind, we now briefly trace the trajectory of Anna Freud's career from its early beginnings, when she worked as a schoolteacher, to the crowning achievements of her child analysis technique, Developmental Lines, Developmental Profiles, and the Hampstead Clinic itself.

In June of 1914, Anna Freud, 18 years old, passed her examinations to begin her apprenticeship as an elementary school teacher, and shortly thereafter the First World War broke out. She apprenticed as a schoolteacher with third, fourth and fifth graders in the school years 1915 to 1916 and 1916 to 1917, that is, in the middle of the war. She was very successful as a teacher, was offered a job, and began to work. But as the war was ending her interests were expanding in the direction of psychoanalysis. In 1918, she attended her first International Psychoanalytical Association Congress in Budapest. Shortly thereafter she began her training analysis with her own father as analyst, and started attending the meetings of the Vienna Psychoanalytic Society (Young-Bruehl, 1988, pp. 64–139).

In 1920, the Spanish Flu swept through Europe and much of the rest of the world, killing tens of millions of people. One of those cut down was Anna Freud's sister Sophie, who at that time had two small boys, Ernst and Heinerle, and was also pregnant with a third. Sophie died along with her baby in utero, and Aunt Anna swooped in and began addressing the two boys' most basic needs for food, clothing, and a stable and caring maternal figure. Then on frequent visits and family vacations, Anna Freud began making her first psychoanalytic interventions to help her nephews with their fears and distress after the loss of their mother. Soon her efforts transformed into a formal analysis of Ernst—the first analysis she ever conducted.

While analysis of family members is regarded as impossible these days, and ill-advised even in those days, we are talking about the early years of analysis when others were also conducting experiments such as these. Karl Abraham, Hermine Hug-Hellmuth, and Melanie Klein, among others, all experimented in analyzing their own family members (Young-Bruehl, 1988, pp. 103–139).

On May 31, 1922, Anna Freud presented her membership paper, "Beating Fantasies and Day Dreams," to the Vienna Psychoanalytic Society (A. Freud, 1922/1974, vol. 1, pp. 137–157). It was a case study built on the theoretical framework of her father's paper, "A Child Is Being Beaten" (1919/1955b).

Anna's patient presented the development of her beating fantasies and daydreams from her early recollections as a five- or six-year-old, an eight- to ten-year-old, and then as they appeared at the time of the analysis when the patient was between fourteen and fifteen years of age (A. Freud, 1922/1974, vol. 1, pp. 142–150). The girl had sexually gratifying erotic beating fantasies of a man beating a boy. Her daydreams, on the other hand, were what she called "nice stories," and not linked directly to erotic pleasure. In the "nice stories," a captured young knight is imprisoned and threatened, but in the end is released in an act of forgiveness, reconciliation, happiness, and pleasure. In both the fantasies and the daydreams, there was always a stronger and a weaker figure.

Over time, the beating theme encroached upon the daydreams and created mixtures of features. In adolescence she began to write down her daydreams,

INTRODUCTION: ANNA FREUD AND HUMBERTO NÁGERA

and this gave her more control over the exciting components. In her paper Anna Freud recalled Siegfried Bernfeld saying that the motivation behind such writing might be attributable to ambitious tendencies originating in the ego, such as a desire to influence others, or to gain respect or love. Anna finished her membership paper with the following statement, "By renouncing her private pleasure in favor of making an impression on others, the author has accomplished an important developmental step: the transformation of an autistic into a social activity. We could say: she has found the road that leads from her fantasy life back to reality" (p. 157). Interestingly, and not incidentally, Elizabeth Young-Bruehl (1988) suggested that the "case" Anna Freud discussed in her membership paper was actually autobiographical, not a clinical case from her practice (p. 104).

Soon Anna Freud was analyzing the children of Dorothy Tiffany Burlingham, an heiress of the Tiffany family of New York, famous for Tiffany jewelry and Tiffany glass. When Anna's friend Eva Rosenfeld began taking in foster-children at her home, Anna Freud referred some of her analytic patients to her, in order to extricate them from emotionally caustic family environments. As the next natural step, Anna Freud, Dorothy Burlingham, and Eva Rosenfeld joined forces to create a private school, the Hietzing School, in Eva Rosenfeld's backyard. Some children attending the school would live in Eva's home and others at their own homes, and most of the children would be in analysis. The main teachers were two young men: Peter Blos and Erik Erikson. After several years of operation, 1926 to 1931, the Hietzing School was closed (Young-Bruehl, 1988, pp. 140–184; Heller, 1992, pp.3–99; Burlingham, 1989, pp. 182–217).

Anna Freud went on analyzing and describing her theoretical discoveries and technical developments in articles and lectures, which developed along the lines of the budding new ego psychology. In fact, she entered the vanguard of ego psychology, along with a large group of Viennese colleagues. Meanwhile in Berlin, another child analyst, Melanie Klein, was gaining a significant following. Klein, heavily influenced by Karl Abraham's emphasis on the vicissitudes of the oral stage, and Sandor Ferenczi's emphasis on the infant's relation to the mother, shortened Freud's schema of libido development from several years into one year. She also emphasized the notion of a normal paranoid-schizoid position in early infancy followed by a normal depressive position, with considerable overlap between the two. Instead of anchoring herself simply to observable behavior for her interpretations, Melanie Klein observed behavior and then drew on clinical experience and theoretical elaborations to incorporate intuitions and speculations into her interpretations of "unconscious phantasies." Thus, while Anna Freud and Melanie Klein both observed children, they looked at them from different perspectives and, naturally, drew different conclusions. Melanie Klein presented her work in England in 1926, and received such an enthusiastic reception that she relocated to London. At that point the tensions between the Vienna School and the Berlin School became the tensions between the Vienna and London schools.

Anna Freud articulated her clinical work and theoretical formulations in *Four Lectures on Child Analysis* in 1927 and the *Theory of Child Analysis* in 1928. As the theories and techniques of Anna Freud and Melanie Klein diverged and elaborated, their professional relations became strained, but their respective works carried on. In 1936 Anna Freud published her landmark, *The Ego and the Mechanisms of Defense*, which, along with Freud's contributions in the 1920s, reoriented psychoanalysis from an 'id psychology' to an 'id, ego and superego psychology,' better known as 'Ego Psychology.' This new Ego Psychology also had important implications for clinical technique.

In February of 1937, Anna Freud and Dorothy Burlingham launched the Edith Jackson Project—a psychoanalytic day-care center for children of poor working-class mothers in Vienna. At the day-care center, the one- and two-year-olds were fed, bathed, clothed, medically examined, and psychoanalytically observed. Anna Freud was interested in instinctual renunciation—the way children renounce the immediate gratification of the pleasure principle and re-orient to the reality principle. She wanted to know if this renunciation took place as a function of development, or if external help was required to restrict the originality and spontaneity of toddlers in order to create the socialized children we recognize in the latency period. One might wonder if this theme was an echo from her autobiographically-based graduation paper pertaining to the renunciation of "private pleasure in favor of making an impression on others."

The staff at the Jackson Nursery included the psychoanalytically trained pediatrician Dr. Josephine Stross, an American analyst named Julia Demming, and a number of volunteers (Burlingham, 1989, pp. 228–229; Molnar, 1992, p. 216). In early February of 1937, Anna Freud wrote to Ernest Jones: "[Paul] Federn told me that Frau Klein will come to Vienna in the spring. I hope she will be interested in the new Kinderheim [the Edith Jackson Project]. In any case I would be happy to show it to her" (Steiner, 2000, p. 83). But with the German Nazi invasion of Austria in March of 1938, the Jackson Nursery came to an abrupt end, and in June, the Freuds went into exile in England, where Melanie Klein had already been established for twelve years.

Anna Freud, her parents, and the extended Freud party arrived in London in June of 1938. In September 1939, Sigmund Freud died, and the Second World War began (Molnar, 1992, pp. 237, 264). It was a time of national emergency, but it was also an opportunity to make a difference both in the lives of children and the theory of psychoanalysis. Anna Freud recalled that after the First World War, her colleagues Siegfried Bernfeld and Willi Hoffer established the Kinderheim Baumgarten—a home and school for Jewish war orphans. It stayed open only six months and basically failed as an institution, but was a crowning success as a model for psychoanalytically-informed residential treatment.

As the Second World War began, London became a target of German rocket bombs, and among the casualties were children orphaned by parents injured or killed in the bombings or parents caught up in the war effort. Anna Freud and Dorothy Burlingham swung into action and set up three homes that offered shelter and stability for 191 children throughout the war. They suffered 593 air raids, including one that left an unexploded 1,000-pound bomb in the next-door neighbor's garden. The nurseries offered a homelike atmosphere, medical treatment, Montessori education, intensive liaison work between the children and their families, and a bomb shelter in which to sleep.

Anna Freud and her colleagues investigated psychological and interpersonal dynamics related to jealousy, attachment, separation, feeding and eating problems, favorite objects, aggression, toilet behavior, sleep disturbances, regression, masturbation, identification, greed, fears, exhibitionism, fantasy, and death. A recurring theme in their investigations was the importance of the mother-child bond and the vicissitudes that bond suffers under wartime conditions (A. Freud, 1939–1945/1973, vol. 3, pp. 4–5, 55, 313, 353–354, 535–536).

Then, with millions of Jews in concentration camps, soldiers at war, and many civilians dedicated to the war effort, something very strange happened—the Anna Freud-Melanie Klein controversies, sometimes referred to as the Psychoanalytic Civil War. The theoretical and technical differences between Anna Freud and Melanie Klein had already been debated for years and there was, from the beginning, a curiously hostile charge to these debates. When Anna Freud and her contingent escaped the Nazis and arrived in London, the Kleinians were far from welcoming. By 1942 the tensions were boiling over between them, and a series of discussions was arranged to evaluate if the Kleinian theory and technique represented a branch of the psychoanalytic tradition, or if it diverged enough to be an alternative theory.

On April 23, 1940, the British analyst James Strachey wrote to his colleague Edward Glover: "My own view is that Mrs. K. has made some highly important contributions to PA [psychoanalysis], but that it's absurd to make out (a) that they cover the whole subject, or (b) that their validity is axiomatic. On the other hand, I think it's equally ludicrous for Miss F. to maintain that PA is a Game Reserve belonging to the F. family and that Mrs. K.'s ideas are totally subversive. These attitudes on both sides are of course purely religious and the antithesis of science" (King & Steiner, 1991, pp. 32–33).

There were distinct differences between the two camps, and in times of peace I am sure it would have been worthwhile to discuss them. But looking back, from the vantage point of the early 21st century, it seems odd that this group of intelligent people could enter into such hot debates on such topics while rocket bombs were literally falling on London. One might even wonder if it was a defensive group strategy to cope with the impotence felt by civilians in the face of war. But in times of peace, a debate such as the one planned would have been worthwhile, as the differences were very real.

INTRODUCTION: ANNA FREUD AND HUMBERTO NÁGERA

Ostensibly the conflict was over theory and technique. Melanie Klein asserted that the Oedipus complex and superego emerge in early infancy, while Anna Freud's observations confirmed her father's view for a later emergence. Melanie Klein believed the transference was present from the beginning of a child analysis, and that it needed to be interpreted as such. Anna Freud maintained that the analyst must cultivate a new and positive relationship with the child analysand, and that the child will not have yet created an "old edition" to transfer onto the analyst. Based on these points of view, Anna Freud asserted the importance of employing educational interventions in the treatment of children, while Melanie Klein advocated a strict analytical approach with deep interpretations articulating primitive fantasies. Melanie Klein asserted that analysis does not harm the ego but actually strengthens it, while Anna Freud believed that the infantile ego is too weak to tolerate classical analysis. Melanie Klein equated a child's play with free association, while Anna Freud noted that play and free association are not equivalent at all. Free association, she pointed out, has the cooperation of an adult psyche trying to enter into a particular kind of dialogue with the analyst, and the child doesn't really have such intentions at all.

Behind these theoretical and technical differences, however, power was at stake. Who was going to represent psychoanalysis? Who was going to teach psychoanalysis? Who were the training analysts going to be? Who would be on the training committee? How were candidates being turned into dutiful soldiers for the Kleinian and Anna Freudian causes?

But just then another problem emerged. Britain was planning on restructuring its health system, and that included mental health. While the Tavistock Clinic had been involved with the community for years and played a significant role in the war effort, the British Psycho-Analytical Society had sidelined itself, and now felt the need to catch up by teaching and training people for the new clinics in post-war England.

But if one was going to teach in the community, would one teach an Anna Freudian psychoanalysis or a Melanie Kleinian psychoanalysis? Though the very "discussions" to determine this had just begun, the external pressure was acute, and suddenly there was a decision to teach in the community before determining which view to present to the public. This decision had the effect of pulling the rug out from underneath the debate, and suddenly the Kleinian viewpoint had been tacitly confirmed as psychoanalytic. The Anna Freudian contingent withdrew from the remaining "discussions." The Kleinian, Freudian, and later, middle-group tracts for training were established, and the tensions between the Anna Freudians and Melanie Kleinians had no clearly defined forum where they could be addressed (A. Freud, 1927/1974, vol. 1, pp. 3–69; Klein, 1932).

In Alex Holder's (2005) examination of the differences between Melanie Klein and Anna Freud, he brought several points into high relief. First, Anna Freud had abandoned the "educational element" she had originally advocated, but replaced it with the importance of offering "developmental help" to assist children with developmental deficits or distortions (pp. 33, 34, 90, 91). And she continued to think it was important for the child analyst to be mindful of the child's external reality at home and at school, as opposed to the exclusively intra-psychic focus of Melanie Klein.

Second, Anna Freud modified her introductory phase of establishing an alliance with the child to one of interpreting the resistance, but she still insisted on the importance of interpreting from the surface and working one's way down, rather than starting off with the interpretation of primitive impulses and fantasies as Melanie Klein advocated (pp. 59, 66). Third, Anna Freud also came to see that children could indeed see the analyst as both a transference object and a new object. But the fact remained for her that the child's transference was different from the transference of an adult, insofar as the child analyst is an active partner in the play, whereas the adult analyst is more of a shadowy figure. Consequently, the child's transference develops differently (pp. 70–72).

Furthermore, Holder came to see that some of the most controversial issues between Melanie Klein and Anna Freud—such as the nature of the child's transference, the onset and nature of the Oedipus complex, and the development of the superego, were not so much disagreements, but differences in definitions. While Anna Freud applied the definitions, developmental sequences, and timetables to these concepts that her father had established, and

INTRODUCTION: ANNA FREUD AND HUMBERTO NÁGERA

which Melanie Klein could also recognize, Klein found it useful to keep the terms, but change the definitions to include various precursors and initial steps in their development (pp. 88, 89, 92, 94–97).

While the differences between Melanie Klein and Anna Freud are very real, the substance of those differences often gave way to a cliquish, my-group-against-your-group attitude that deeply affected training and the social and professional interactions among analysts. It was a case of what Sigmund Freud would have called "the narcissism of minor differences."

But even after considering the psychoanalytic civil war as a defensive strategy of a group trying to deal with the feelings of impotence in the face of war, as a way of managing the underlying power dynamics of the British Psycho-Analytic Society, or even as an expression of the narcissism of minor differences, there still remained some very real divergent psychoanalytic viewpoints that had to be dealt with. And since there was no longer a common forum in which to work things out, the two groups dedicated themselves to research, which, consciously or unconsciously, addressed the very differences they had been discussing for decades—their different views of early child development.

The war ended in Europe on May 8, 1945, and 732 Jewish orphans who had survived the concentration camps were sent to England for care, education, and adoption. After Anna Freud's war nurseries were closed, a number of the young people who worked with her sought further training as psychologists or psychiatric social workers—training that would allow them to work in the child guidance clinics and homes for Jewish war orphans that were then springing up all across Great Britain. As these young people went to work in these clinics and homes, Anna Freud offered training seminars and supervision. In England 28 homes for the child survivors of concentration camps were set up as foster-home environments, beginning in 1945 until the children were taken in by their extended families, adopted by other families, or were old enough to go out on their own and find work.

One group of child survivors of the concentration camps was cared for at Weir Courtney House, a home run by Alice Goldberger (Bateson, 2010, pp. 1–3), and another group was given a home at Bulldogs Bank, run by Sophie and Gertrude Dann. These three women and others participated in seminars and supervision with Anna Freud as they ministered to the personal wounds of child victims of the holocaust. Anna Freud and the Dann sisters later wrote an article on their difficult and very important work at Bulldogs Bank (A. Freud, 1951/1968, vol. 4, pp. 163–229). Later when the Hampstead Clinic was established, concentration camp survivors found analytic treatment available to them.

The seminars and supervision that Anna Freud offered the young people who worked in the clinics and homes in post-war Great Britain were formalized in 1947 as the Hampstead Child-Therapy Course. Training included lectures, seminars, and personal analyses for the candidates. Clinical work was undertaken offsite (Sandler, 1965, pp. 109–123).

In February 1952, generous donations enabled Anna Freud and her colleagues to buy a building with treatment rooms. And with the reality of a physical space established, the Hampstead Child-Therapy Course became the Hampstead Child-Therapy Course and Clinic, with Anna Freud as director, Dr. Liselotte Frankl as psychiatrist-in-charge, and Drs. Augusta Bonnard, Josephine Stross, and Willi Hoffer as consultants (Sandler, 1965, pp. 109–123; Kennedy, 1978).

In 1956, Sigmund Freud's centenary, Anna Freud was 60 years old and entering a phase in her life characterized by blazing productivity. Her Clinic was up and running, donations were coming in, and psychoanalysis was enjoying its Golden Age. The Clinic was serving the community, child analysts were being trained, the Clinic was involved in multiple research projects, and the staff was prolific in its contributions to the psychoanalytic literature.

In the following years, the Hampstead Clinic opened two other houses, and changed its name to the Hampstead Centre for the Psychoanalytic Study and Treatment of Children (Sandler, 1965, pp. 109–123; Kennedy, 1978; Friedmann, 1988, pp. 277–278).

Those involved in the Anna Freud-Melanie Klein controversies of the early 1940s tried subsequently to come to terms with the fact that the two groups were observing child development in very different ways. The Anna Freudians observed the slower development of the libido and the various intermediary stages in the development of the ego and superego. The Kleinians, on the

INTRODUCTION: ANNA FREUD AND HUMBERTO NÁGERA

other hand, saw development moving much quicker, and the early appearance of fully-developed aspects of psychological structure. Though I don't believe there was any conscious intention to sort out the Freud-Klein controversies through research, the fact of the matter is that both sides dedicated themselves to child observation, infant observation, child analysis and various research projects, where, among other things, their disagreements could, in a sense, be explored.

It was into this rather exciting environment that a 31-year-old Cuban psychiatrist, Humberto Nágera, arrived in London to begin his psychoanalytic training. Nágera has always had a large capacity for work, a quality that appealed very much to Anna Freud. In Cuba he had gone to school and trained to be a psychiatrist while at the same time running a construction company, from which he was able to earn enough to pay for his education, start his family, and fund his analytic training in London. He began his training at the Institute of the British Psycho-Analytical Society in 1958, and then in 1959, he began taking additional seminars and took on child cases for training in child analysis, at the Hampstead Clinic.

There has been, throughout the history of psychoanalysis, an unending problem with the confusion of terms and their multiple definitions. It began with Adler, continued with Jung, and became a topic of concern with many new theorists, including Melanie Klein. In the 1960s a psychoanalytic Concept Group was established at the Hampstead Clinic, led by Humberto Nágera. Their work was to research the Core Psychoanalytic Concepts, as Sigmund Freud had presented and developed them during the course of his life. The work of the Concept Group provided clear theoretical descriptions and offered discriminating readers the opportunity to study the ideas of Freud in a concise and historically-based presentation.

While Klein shortened Freud's view of child development from several years into just the first year of life, Anna Freud introduced her Lines of Development, which marked the difference between earlier, middle, and later stages of development. The concept of Developmental Lines traced the progression from dependence to emotional self-reliance and adult object-relatedness; from suckling to rational eating; from wetting and soiling to bladder and bowel control; from irresponsibility to responsibility in body management; from egocentricity to companionship; from body to toy; and from play to work. The Developmental Lines, as I understand them, are normative paths around which one assesses the psychological structure and functioning of a child in order to understand pathology and to plan treatment (A. Freud, 1965).

And with the Lines of Development came the Developmental Profiles. These Developmental Profiles provide a schema to assess personality structure metapsychologically. They were designed for babies, toddlers, children, adolescents, adults, blind children and deaf children. The Personality Profiles allow the clinician to assess the difference between fully formed psychological structures as well as their prototypes, precursors, antecedents, and forerunners in early infancy.

In 1965 Joseph Sandler presented the Hampstead Clinic point of view, clearly reiterating one of the critical differences between Anna Freud and Melanie Klein (Sandler, 1965, pp. 112–113; Moran, 1988, p. 263). Anna Freud spoke of the importance of introducing into child analyses the educative measures, developmental help, and direct involvement with the child's external environment. Melanie Klein, on the other hand, minimized these efforts, as she thought they were not analytic, and not necessary. Sandler wrote:

> [In] both our diagnostic and our therapeutic work with children we are primarily interested in the ways in which the child has departed from the normal course of development, and in the possibilities of restoring the child to a developmental path that will ensure his progression through all the stages necessary for successful adaptation. The therapeutic approach adopted is therefore oriented towards removing, as far as possible, the hindrances to progressive development and adaptation. Many of these hindrances lie in the child's social and physical environment, and where it is possible to achieve the appropriate changes in the external situation through advice to the parents, through the work of the psychoanalytically oriented social worker, or through nursery school education, this is the method of choice. But in this connection the assessment of the degree to which the child has

INTRODUCTION: ANNA FREUD AND HUMBERTO NÁGERA

"internalized" such external conflict is crucial. If a substantial degree of internalization has taken place and an internal neurotic conflict has replaced conflict with the external environment, then the orientation of our treatment shifts from work with the child's environment to the treatment of the child himself, and here the method of choice is psychoanalytic child therapy. (Sandler, 1965, pp. 112–113)

The Hampstead Child-Therapy Course and Clinic in 1965 offered training in child analysis, psychological evaluations and therapy for children, a nursery school, a special nursery school for blind children, a well-baby clinic, discussion groups for nursery school teachers, discussion groups with pediatric consultants, liaison work with the pediatric unit at a general hospital, and lectures to professional organizations. They were doing research at the Hampstead Clinic on diagnostic problems and devising strategies for creating personality profiles of people at different developmental stages. They also did research on the development of blind children; the analyses of adolescents; the dynamics of delinquency; simultaneous analyses of mother-child pairs; analyses of borderline and psychotic children; the Hampstead Psychoanalytic Index for recording observations in the nursery school and in analyses; the psychoanalytic concept group; a clinical concept group, and much more (Sandler, 1965, pp. 109–123). Anna Freud's *Normality and Pathology in Childhood: Assessments of Development* was published in 1965. It brought together the findings of 45 years of clinical and theoretical work. After 1966 the Hampstead Clinic concentrated its efforts on children from underprivileged and disadvantaged families. By 1978 the training program had already graduated more than one hundred child analysts (A. Freud, 1988, p. 265; Kennedy, 1978; Friedmann, 1988, pp. 277–278). Anna Freud received many honors during her lifetime including honorary degrees from Clark University (1950), Jefferson Medical College (1946), University of Chicago (1964), Sheffield University (1966), Yale University (1968) and University of Vienna (1975). She was also granted the title C.B.E.—Commander of the British Empire—at Buckingham Palace in 1967. In addition to her eight volumes of collected works on psychoanalysis there are her other contributions such as *In The Best Interest of the Child*

(1986), *Beyond the Best Interest of the Child* (1973) and *Before the Best Interests of the Child* (1979) which were co-authored by Joseph Goldstein, Albert J. Solnit and Sonja Goldstein. These three books contributed to a revolution in the legal handling of custody battles in the United States.

Dr. Humberto Nágera was at Hampstead Clinic from 1959 to 1968. During that time he went from being a trainee to Anna Freud's right-hand man, and before announcing his departure Anna Freud asked him to be her heir apparent and take over the directorship of the Clinic. While honored by Miss Freud's trust and confidence, Nágera chose to immigrate to the United States in order to secure a financially stable future for his wife and children, and also for his parents who, as mentioned in the Foreword, became dependent on him after they were forced to leave communist Cuba.

Saying goodbye to Nágera was not easy for Anna Freud, but she understood his rationale completely, as she had also looked after her parents. After leaving the Hampstead Clinic, Humberto Nágera carried on the spirit of Anna Freud and the tradition of the Hampstead Clinic in his work as Director of the Children's Psychiatric Hospital at the University of Michigan Medical Center, as a training analyst at the Michigan Psychoanalytic Society, and later as professor of psychiatry at the University of South Florida and as Director of the Carter-Jenkins Center in Tampa, Florida. Though they were no longer working together after 1968, the bond of friendship between Anna Freud and Humberto Nágera remained strong, and their correspondence continued up until the time of Anna Freud's final illness.

The book before you contains Anna Freud's letters to Humberto Nágera during the course of this extraordinary collaboration (1959–1980), which was one of the most productive phases in Anna Freud's life. It also includes related documents such as grant reports, Anna Freud's notes on articles Nágera had written, and a few letters from others, which are related to Anna Freud and Humberto Nágera's work together. Also included are Anna Freud's forewords to several of Nágera's books, and a transcription of Anna Freud's discussion of

INTRODUCTION: ANNA FREUD AND HUMBERTO NÁGERA

obsessional neurosis, which she delivered on a panel moderated by Humberto Nágera at the 1965 International Psychoanalytical Association Congress in Amsterdam. The collection of letters ends with some poignant letters from Nágera's friend and colleague W. Ernest Freud, Anna Freud's nephew and the only Freud grandchild to become a psychoanalyst. The final document in the series is a letter from Anna Freud to a fourteen-year-old boy who wanted to know what qualities a person should have to pursue a career as a psychoanalyst.

Through these letters and related documents we get an insider's view of psychoanalysis, not as a static monolithic dogma, but as a dynamic human tradition, embedded in personal relationships, and passed on from one generation to the next.

Anna Freud's Letters to Humberto Nágera and Related Documents

For ease of reading, all dates have been changed to the format of month, date, and year, i.e., September 21, 1959. Additionally, Anna Freud did not sign her name "Anna Freud" but rather as "Annafreud." This spelling has been preserved in the transcription of these letters. Underlining and italics have been left intact as they appear in the original documents. Illegible writing has naturally been omitted and the patients mentioned have been given pseudonyms. People toward whom Anna Freud was critical, in her confidential correspondence to Nágera, have been given pseudonyms as well. It was not her intention to hurt them and I don't wish to either.

D.B.

DOCUMENT 1   ANNA FREUD

20 Maresfield Gardens [1]
London

September 21, 1959

Dear Dr. Nágera,

If Dr. Hoffer [2] agrees, we shall be very glad to have you as a guest at our weekly Staff Conference [3], on Wednesdays at 2 p.m. I hope that you will enjoy the occasions.

Yours sincerely
Annafreud [4]

1. 20 Maresfield Gardens was Anna Freud's home in the Hampstead district of London. When Sigmund Freud left Vienna under the threat of the Nazis in June 1938, he and his wife Martha, daughter Anna, sister-in-law Minna Bernays, and housekeeper Paula Fichtl settled, at first, into a home at 39 Elsworthy Road in London. On September 30, 1938, they moved into 20 Maresfield Gardens. Freud died there in September 1939, and Anna Freud lived there for the rest of her life with her close friend and colleague, Dorothy Burlingham and their house maid, Paula Fichtl. On Freud's centennial in May 1956, the London County Council placed a plaque on the front of the building, recognizing it at as the home of the "Founder of Psychoanalysis" from 1938 to 1939. It later received a second plaque recognizing it as the home of Anna Freud, "Pioneer in Child Psychoanalysis," from 1938 to 1982. And in 1986 the Freud home was transformed into the Freud Museum, London.
2. Dr. Wilhelm "Willi" Hoffer (1897–1967) was Humberto Nágera's analyst. Dr. Hoffer had a Ph.D. in philosophy (1922), as well as a medical degree (1929). A protégé of Siegfried Bernfeld, Hoffer worked with him on the Kinderheim Baumgarten (a home for Jewish war orphans after the First World War). Hoffer trained as a psychoanalyst in the early 1920s, was analyzed by Hermann Nunberg, and soon became a training analyst. He worked closely with Anna Freud, Siegfried Bernfeld, and August Aichhorn in the formulation of psychoanalytic pedagogy. With Ernest Jones's help, he immigrated to London in 1938 and was a staunch supporter of Anna Freud during the "controversies" between her and Melanie Klein. Hoffer was editor of the *International Journal of Psychoanalysis* from 1949 to 1959, and the author of a small book, *Psychoanalysis: Practical and Research Aspects* (1955) (King & Steiner, 1991, pp. xiv–xiv). In England lay analysts needed to have coverage from a physician in order to practice. Hoffer, with an M.D., provided physician coverage for both Anna Freud and Dorothy Burlingham.
3. The Wednesday Weekly Staff Conferences were special meetings for the Senior Staff, which were held in 20 Maresfield Gardens.

4. Nágera recalled: "Anna Freud was shy. It didn't look like it because she was such a good speaker. Of course, if you met her, she would be very appropriate. But in reality her character was that of a shy person, partly because the Freuds had been burned many times by newspaper people that interviewed them, then distorted things. So they were rather reticent, that way, but very friendly. Miss Freud was a wonderful person. She couldn't have been better, really. I knew Anna Freud reasonably well. I was pretty close to her. I remember some of the work we did together. There were a lot of projects at the Clinic. One of them for example concerned the study and analytic treatment of people that had been in concentration camps."

―⁂―

DOCUMENT 2   ANNA FREUD

20 Maresfield Gardens
London

March 15, 1960

Dr. Humberto Nágera,
42 Southwood Ave.
London N.6. [1]

Dear Dr. Nágera,

As I promised you, we have discussed your training problems [2] among us, and Dr. Ilse Hellman [3] promised to discuss the result with you. I hope she will do so soon.

Yours sincerely,
Annafreud

1. Humberto Nágera's address in London.

2. The "training problems" were mentioned in Dr. Nágera's foreword and are further described in the first annotation under the next letter.
3. Ilse Hellman was one of Nágera's supervisors. Nágera recalled: "Ilse Hellman was from Vienna and she came from a very distinguished family of diplomats and she got interested in psychoanalysis and became a very bright, brilliant I would say, analyst. She supervised one of my adolescent cases and I attended many of her lectures and seminars. She was very bright and her knowledge of adolescents was remarkable. Her abilities as an analyst and a clinician were also remarkable. She was very close to Anna Freud and they worked together for a very, very long time and unfortunately she died a few years ago. She was an actual presence at the Clinic and somebody that Anna Freud trusted and thought the world of. She was a very reliable person and a very good human being."

DOCUMENT 3   ANNA FREUD

20 Maresfield Gardens
London

October 23, 1960

Dear Dr. Nágera,

Please excuse the delay in my answer to your letter. There were so many questions to solve after my return, and additionally I lost quite a few days through being out of commission with flu.

I appreciate all the difficulties of your present situation [1], and I am extremely sorry that you will not be able to carry our [out] your original plan of training fully for child analysis. I hope that being in the Clinic [2] will give you at least some orientation in the field.

As regards paid work for the Index [3], I think we can arrange for that, even if only to a modest amount. Perhaps we can have a word about that during the week. So far we have never employed a trained psychiatrist on the research side of the work, and I have to find out what the appropriate payment per session would be.

Yours sincerely
Annafreud

1. With regard to the "present situation" Nágera recalled: "I was in clinical training and after the first four or five months of my being in England, Castro came to power in Cuba and I got some menacing letters from the government saying that I had to send my family back—that means, my wife and my children—otherwise they wouldn't allow my money to come through. This was not government money, this was my money. I saw this and, of course, I wanted to finish the training. At that point it was not known that what was happening in Cuba was a communist development. I was in analysis, and Willie Hoffer really helped me. He said, "Dr. Nágera, you do what you want but if you send your family, you will never see them again." I said, "Well, what do you mean?" And he said, "Well that's a totalitarian style of government. I don't know what is happening there but it's not what it looks like. That's a totalitarian attitude. You send your family back and you will never see them again. They are not going to send you your money or anything. That is it." And so that made me think. Because, of course, Hoffer, being a Jew, had similar experiences of a much more horrendous kind. He lost most of his family in concentration camps. But he knew totalitarian things very well, and I didn't. So he opened my eyes and I said, "Well then I'm not going to send anybody anywhere. I'll stay here and see what I'll do." And it was difficult because I had gone to England with a student permit, which meant I couldn't work for money. So I had to change all that." I had no money even to feed my

family, pay the rent, etc. I could not pay Hoffer for my analysis but he agreed to continue, and let me pay him later, which I did, but I could not pay for supervisors, for the child analysis training, the fee for the Institute, etc. My adult supervisors had either waived the fee or let me pay later whenever I could. I was in fact considering moving to Canada or Australia, where they needed M.D.s and were hiring. I only had a student visa in London, so I could not be employed by anyone. Miss Freud did not want me to leave and was trying to help. Luckily Jenny Waelder-Hall, another good analyst friend of Anna from Vienna and a big name at the Washington Institute, came to visit, and I was to teach her about the Developmental Profile. Her husband, who had been a member of the old League of Nations, came with her. When Jenny learned about my situation, she arranged for me to talk to him. When he saw the menacing letters I had received from the Castro government, he said he could get me political asylum in England as he had good connections in the British government from his time in the League of Nations. He was an Australian, and within two or three weeks I was given residence in England, which permitted me to work, and Miss Freud hired me for the Clinic. It ended this horrific time, and at least I could feed my family, pay the rent, etc. Gloria, my wife, had lost about 15 pounds by then, because whatever little food we could get she gave to the children. I did not know that because I was working at the Clinic where I could get some food free."

2. The "Clinic" was a short way of referring to The Hampstead Child-Therapy Course and Clinic.
3. The "Index" refers to the Hampstead Psychoanalytic Index, a catalogue of indexed clinical observations. It was started in 1954 under Dorothy Burlingham, but observations were being recorded on index cards long before that in the war nurseries, and the Jackson Nursery in Vienna. When Manna Friedmann and her colleagues asked how these notes should be written, Anna Freud replied, "Make a note of anything you would feel inclined to tell a friend, either because it charmed you, or it

was funny and amused you, or it was irritating and angered you; make a note of anything which would confirm some psychoanalytic theory or which would contradict it; and make a note of any behavior which would seem to you precocious or the opposite" (Friedmann, 1988, pp. 280–281). Later, Joseph Sandler took charge of the Hampstead Psychoanalytic Index.

DOCUMENT 4   ANNA FREUD

20 Maresfield Gardens
London

March 17, 1961

Dear Dr. Nágera,

May I ask you to give this letter [1] great attention and to answer it as fully as it is possible for you.

We are on the point of making an important new application [2] to the National Institute of Health in the United States for a grant to our Clinic which is meant to substitute for several other grants which will terminate in the near future. This application is of special importance to the clinic and to Dr. Eissler [3] since we hope that it may relieve him and us of many financial worries which might arise otherwise. The application will be made for a comprehensive research plan on diagnostic work, using the clinical and theoretical information which comes from all parts of the Clinic. Therefore not only those directly engaged in diagnosis but workers from various parts of the Clinic will be included in it and have to be described by me in rather elaborate biographical sketches. As you know, we have biographical material from many of you already for former applications but they will not be sufficient for this one.

May I ask you therefore to fill in the enclosed questionnaire and to send me any items for point 4, "supplemental information" of which you can think. Please do not forget anything which is to your own credit and therefore also of credit to us. And, please add to your degrees, or employments the dates which belong to them. Whatever cannot be put into the form itself under the first three points will go under "supplemental information." Whatever former work you can mention, which is even remotely connected with the assessment of childhood disturbances, will be of use. Please, also add any publications that you have brought out in connection with the Clinic work or formerly.

p.t.o.

I shall be very grateful to have your answer soon.

Yours sincerely,
Annafreud

Enclosure [4]

1. This was a letter sent to all members of the staff at the Clinic.
2. This was an application for a large grant from the National Institute of Mental Health in the United States. The Hampstead Clinic, and the War Nurseries before it, were always supported by grant monies from foundations in the United States. These were sometimes small and sometimes larger, but the hunt for new grants and donations was a frequent concern. With this particular grant they hoped to get for the Hampstead Clinic a tremendous amount of treatment and research financially covered for an extended period of time.
3. Dr. Kurt Eissler (1908–1999) was a Viennese analyst, psychoanalytic historian, distinguished clinician, and founder of the Sigmund Freud Archives. He was a close friend of Anna Freud and very active in fund raising for the Hampstead Clinic (Young-Bruhl, 1988, p. 339).
4. Enclosure not available.

DOCUMENT 5   ANNA FREUD

Tresco [1]

May 4, 1961

Dear Dr. Nágera,

Thank you for sending me Eddie's [2] reports. I am very glad that you have kept them confidential and I would much rather not have them go through the usual Clinic channels. They can remain in your and mine [sic] files.

Poor Eddie! I hope Mr. Singer [3] will convince the mother that she has to give him the chance to speak openly about his resentment concerning her affairs in his analysis, by asking you to introduce the subject openly. If she does not do that, then he is quite right to steal, and it is she who spoils his chances in analysis. Children are only too logical.

I enjoy this holiday very much.

Yours sincerely
Annafreud

1. Tresco is the second largest island of the Isles of Scilly in Cornwall, England.
2. Nágera recalled: "Eddie [pseudonym] was my under-five child training case at the Clinic supervised by Mrs. Hedwig Hoffer, Willi Hoffer's wife. Eddie's mother was a young woman married to an older man and she was extremely promiscuous in ways that could not escape the child's observation. For example, she would seduce the mailman, get him in the house and have intercourse with him, etc. She was referred to an analyst by the name of Mr. Singer."
3. Mr. Singer is also pseudonym for an analyst at the Clinic. Pseudonym used to avoid any additional identifying data of the patient.

DOCUMENT 6   ANNA FREUD

20 Maresfield Gardens
London

June 27, 1961

Dear Dr. Nágera,

So far there is no answer from Dr. Muriel Gardiner [1], but I expect it confidently.
Thank you for your letter of June 20th concerning Eddie. I find the situation, as you describe it, very bad indeed and, besides, it makes me quite angry [2]. What these parents actually do is to leave the work about the child's well-being to us while they act as they like. They do everything to harm the child and then expect us to undo the harm. That seems unfair and, besides, it cannot be done. Should one really continue an analysis under such conditions?

Yours sincerely,
Annafreud

1. Dr. Muriel Gardiner (1901–1985) was an American psychoanalyst and close friend of Anna Freud. She was a wealthy heiress to the Morris and Co. meat packing business on her father's side and the Swift and Co. meat packing business on her mother's side. She studied medicine and psychoanalysis in Vienna where she entered Anna Freud's circle and in the mid–1930s, became very active in the anti-Fascist Austrian underground in which she risked her life and ended up saving hundreds of Jews from the terrors of Nazism. The popular film "Julia" was based on her work in the Austrian underground. She was a psychoanalyst affiliated with the Philadelphia Psychoanalytic Society.
2. Nágera recalled: "At Hampstead one wrote weekly summaries of one's patients that were sent to Miss Freud. She read them all and would frequently send back a comment."

DOCUMENT 7   ANNA FREUD

August 27, 1961

Dear Dr. Nágera,

Thank you very much for sending me your paper on the Profile [1]. I think it is excellent and I found it exciting to read. You grasped all the implications of the problem and carried them where they ought to be carried; that is a rare thing to do. I liked quite especially your remarks on the "age-adequate responses" where I always grope for the right expressions and have difficulty to find them; also your reasoning at the end concerning the internal conflicts between the drives and your description of their dependence on the outcome of the oedipal identifications; and equally your insistence that thinking has to proceed from the material to the headings and not vice versa.

There are a few points that I would like to discuss with you in detail still, when I am in London again, where some amendments might be useful.

The whole thing will be most useful for internal use. For external use: what would you think if we published a paper on it together? I could do the introductory thoughts that led to the setting up of the Profile and then your part comes in as the application of it [2]. I am sure the Ps.A. [Psychoanalytic] Study of the Child [3] would be glad to publish it.

Dr. Marianne Kris [4], who has been reading the finished Profiles all summer, will be in 20 Maresfield Gardens for 2 ½ days from 30th August onwards. She would like very much to ask you a number of questions concerning the work, and I gave her your telephone number.

Now for a different matter: I had the enclosed letter concerning you from the Newland Foundation and I think you should write them a letter right now. Perhaps you could best do it in the following way: 1) describe your situation; 2) ask for the adequate grant to continue your analysis; 3) if this should seem too much for them, ask alternatively for a sum as additional living-grant [5].

I hope it will all work out very well.

Yours sincerely
Annafreud

1. The "Profile," mentioned here, was a short way of referring to the Developmental Profile, about which Nágera had written. The Developmental Profile is a diagnostic schema based on a metapsychological way of thinking and way of organizing clinical material that Anna Freud had outlined in her New York lectures in 1960, titled "Four Contributions to the Psychoanalytic Study of the Child." In contrast to a symptom-focused approach, the diagnostic personality profile is neither a psychological test nor a questionnaire. It is a framework for a comprehensive assessment of the patient, based on both clinical and nonclinical observations. Its aim is to call the therapist's attention to all aspects of the personality so that the evaluation is not skewed in one direction or another, but rather addresses the metapsychology of the whole personality. It organizes one's thinking about the patient's ego, id, superego, libido, aggression, fixation points, etc. It started out informally under the direction of Dr. Lisolette Frankl and Renate Putzel, and when it became more formally organized, Humberto Nágera took over the chairmanship of the Profile Research Group.
2. There were many articles generated by the Profile Research Group, but the one that Anna Freud refers to here is one that was later published as chapter one, "The Developmental Profile," in Nágera's *The Developmental Approach to Child Psychopathology* (1981). New York: Jason Aronson, Inc., pp. 3–35.
3. *The Psychoanalytic Study of the Child* is a book-sized annual dedicated to psychoanalysis and children. It was the post-war English version of the *Zeitschrift für Psychoanalytische Pädagogik* (Young-Bruehl, 1988, p. 159). The founding editors were Anna Freud, Heinz Hartmann, and Ernst Kris. Many of the main editors were also close associates of Anna Freud.
4. Dr. Marianne Kris (1900–1980) was born Marianne Rie, the daughter of Dr. Oscar Rie, Anna Freud's pediatrician and a close personal friend of Sigmund Freud. Marianne Rie became a medical doctor and then psychiatrist in 1925, and did her psychoanalytic training in Germany. She and Anna Freud became close personal friends. She married the art

historian and psychoanalyst Ernst Kris and later moved to New York, where she practiced for many years.
5. Nágera recalled, "This was a grant to continue paying for my analysis, supervisors, etc."

DOCUMENT 8   ANNA FREUD

Far End
Walberswick [1]

September 12, 1961

Dear Dr. Nágera,

Today I had a personal letter from Muriel Gardiner in which she excuses herself for the indirect answer to my last one. But she assures me that Mr. Sklar [2] of the New Land Foundation [3] is fully informed about you and that there is a very good chance that you will get a grant.

I pass it on since it seems good news to me.

Yours sincerely
Annafreud

1. Far End was the name of Anna Freud and Dorothy Burlingham's beach house in a village called Walberswick, 120 miles away from London, in Suffolk. They retreated there for vacations from their work at the Hampstead Clinic, but it was also sometimes used as a place to write. Irene Freud, the wife of Anna Freud's nephew, W. Ernest Freud, recalled in her memoirs (1990) that, "The village itself was frequented by artists because of the wonderful quality of the light, the openness of the landscape with its gorse and heather-covered common land, its windmill, its estuary and fishing boats, and its sea marshes where reeds still grow and are harvested for thatching. A colony of herons used to nest in the trees

outside the village each year, and there is a wide variety of bird life... [Far End had] a large garden and wonderful views across the fields and shoreline. The garden had an extensive lawn protected from the east winds by trees, bushes, and shrubs and there were many small hidden alcoves where one could sit and chat in private."
2. Mr. Sklar was probably an administrator of the New Land Foundation.
3. Nágera recalled: "The New Land Foundation was a private foundation originally sponsored by Muriel Gardiner, an analyst and old friend of Anna who very much helped the clinic with funds. She was very wealthy having inherited a huge fortune. She was a generous, extraordinarily kind lady."

DOCUMENT 9   ANNA FREUD

20 Maresfield Gardens
London

March 24, 1962

Dear Dr. Nágera,

I look forward to being in the Clinic again this week.

Please, do not let us forget to discuss your remark about auto-erotism [1] which puzzled me so much when you made it after Dr. Sandler's [2] presentation. I find it minuted also by Dr. Holder [3], but surely there must be a misunderstanding. Did you mean that in the Three Essays [4] and up to 1923 auto-erotism was considered to take the place of object-relationship, or that it was considered to exist besides object-relations? If you had meant the former, what about the Oedipus complex and the whole of the child's early love-life?

I cannot make it out.

Yours sincerely
Annafreud

1. Regarding auto-erotism, Nágera recalled: "I don't really know what she was referring to in this letter. I wrote and published a paper titled Autoerotism, autoerotic activities and ego development (*The Developmental Approach to Child Psychopathology* (1981). New York: Jason Aronson, pp. 111–127), where I discussed Freud's development of these concepts through the years. He, in fact, described three different types of autoerotic activities. The first, during the phase of autoerotism, the second during the phase of primary narcissism, and finally autoerotic activities during the phase of object relations. There are some similarities as well as significant differences between these autoerotic activities during these three phases. It is an interesting and important but a very neglected issue."
2. Dr. Joseph Sandler (1927–1998), born in Cape Town, South Africa, was an excellent student who obtained his Ph.D. in England at 23, and immediately began his parallel psychoanalytic training and medical studies. He completed his analytic training in 1952, when he was 25. He worked at the Hampstead Clinic, where he was in charge of the Hampstead Index Project. He wrote voluminously and served two terms as president of the International Psychoanalytical Association (Fonagy, 2001, pp. 815–817).
3. Dr. Alex Holder (1931-) was a member of the Hampstead Clinic team from 1960 to 1983. In addition to other important publications, he is the author of *Anna Freud, Melanie Klein, and the Psychoanalysis of Children and Adolescents* (2005).
4. "Three Essays" refers to Sigmund Freud's important book, *Three Essays Toward a Theory of Sexuality* (1905/1953).

DOCUMENT 10   ANNA FREUD

[It is likely the following undated letter precedes or follows the next letter.]

Dear Dr. Nágera,

I am very grateful for all the trouble you have taken about the diagnosis quotations [1]. If the sending is not too much trouble I would very much like to have the cards since *Ego and Id* [2] out here, to study as a sample. What I am after are contributions to a number of questions such as: infantile neurosis versus adult neurosis; differential diagnosis between neurosis, psychosis, borderline-states, character neurosis, character formation, prognosis, and prediction.

I look forward to discussing all sorts of things when I am back in London.

With appreciation and thanks,
Yours sincerely
Annafreud

1. Anna Freud was enlisting Nágera's assistance in studying some basic psychoanalytic concepts regarding diagnosis as Sigmund Freud had discussed them throughout his collected works.
2. Anna Freud was looking for quotations from Freud regarding diagnosis "since" or after *The Ego and the Id* was published in 1923.

DOCUMENT 11   ANNA FREUD

Far End
Walberswick

May 9, 1962

Dear Dr. Nágera,

Thank you very much for the cards [1] which I am reading with great interest. I feel very guilty, though, that you have typed them yourself.

I do want the earlier ones also if you could sort them out for being typed. There must be a great deal of importance contained in the case histories (specially Little Hans and Rat Man [2]); on the other hand the divisions of neuroses in the Fleiss [3] letters and in the early papers (Anxiety Neuroses, etc.) would not be applicable anymore, though they are historically very important.

I revise the translation of the New Introductory Lectures [4] for Mr. Strachey [5] now, and I find re-reading the text as fascinating (and as new) as ever.

With thanks,
yours sincerely
Annafreud

1. With regard to the "cards," Dr. Nágera recalled: "We collected, and wrote on cards, Freud's statements on the subject of diagnosis, all through his life. Miss Freud needed them for something she was writing. I had assigned the job to Mrs. Neurath, an old child analyst that was a member of the Concept Research Group that I headed. Her handwriting was difficult to read so I decide to type them myself before sending them to Anna Freud.
2. Little Hans is the pseudonym Freud gave for a child whose analysis was conducted by Freud's colleague, Max Graf (the child's father), under Freud's supervision. The Rat Man is the pseudonym Freud gave to one of his adult patients. (See Sigmund Freud (1909/1955). *Two Case*

Histories: "Little Hans" and the "Rat Man." In James Strachey (Ed. & Trans.), *Standard Edition*, Vol. 10.
3. Dr. Wilhelm Fleiss (1858–1928) was an otolaryngologist in Berlin and a close personal friend of Freud's in the late 1800s when Freud was formulating his theory and technique of dream interpretation. After an intense personal association there followed a cooling of relations and an end to the friendship.
4. "New Introductory Lectures" refers to Freud's *New Introductory Lectures on Psycho-analysis* published in 1933, which James Strachey was translating into English for the *Standard Edition of the Complete Psychological Works of Sigmund Freud* in the early 1960s.
5. James Strachey (1887–1967) was a British psychoanalyst and the lead translator, along with his wife Alix Strachey, of *Standard Edition of the Complete Psychological Works of Sigmund Freud*.

DOCUMENT 12 ANNA FREUD

September 7, 1962

Dear Dr. Nágera,

Thank you very much for the Profiles [1]. I think they are very well chosen. Unluckily the copies of Hank, Paul, Maggie, and Donna, are such bad ones [2] that I cannot take them to America as they are. But I hope to find better ones in No. 20 Maresfield Gardens when I come home on the 10th. If not, we have to hunt up the first copies which, after all, must be somewhere.

I have done a chapter for one diagnostic report, to follow yours, since it is also introductory. It is called "Diagnostic Skills and their Growth in Psycho-Analysis" [3]. It can be copied only after I come back from America but I shall bring it to the Diagnostic Group on the 11th.

Thank you also for the set of Mrs. Neurath's cards. I have sent on her Note to James Strachey for his opinion; I think she is quite right, probably. The cards are very interesting for a historical study of the diagnostic concepts.

For the present purpose, of course, they might be confusing since the readers would think that we do not distinguish between past and present.

As for the Outline for your Seminar [4], I cannot see that you missed out on anything. Perhaps, in spite of the libido-theory coming into being long before the theory of aggression, it would be useful to establish some connecting links with the latter. I see that you have such links in mind anyway under point 5) so far as object relations and ego developments are concerned (when you talk of "phases").

Best regards,
yours sincerely
Annafreud

1. The Developmental Profile is a diagnostic tool that Anna Freud created for work with children. Subsequent articles elaborating this work and applying the Developmental Profile to other populations are:
   Anna Freud (1962). Assessment of childhood disturbances. *Psychoanalytic Study of the Child*, 17:149–158.
   Anna Freud, Humberto Nágera and W. Ernest Freud (1965). Metapsychological assessment of the adult personality: The adult profile. *Psychoanalytic Study of the Child*, 20: 9–41.
   Moses Laufer (1965). Assessment of adolescent disturbances: The application of Anna Freud's Diagnostic Profile. *Psychoanalytic Study of the Child*, 20:99–123.
   W. E. Freud. (1967). Assessment of early infancy: Problems and considerations. (Also known as The Baby Profile–Part I). *Psychoanalytic Study of the Child*, 22:216–238.
   ——— (1971). The Baby Profile–Part II. *Psychoanalytic Study of the Child*, 26:172–194.
   Dorothy Burlingham (1975). Special problems of blind infants: Blind baby profile. *Psychoanalytic Study of the Child*, 30: 3–13.
   Paul Brinich (1981). Application of the metapsychological profile to the assessment of deaf children. *Psychoanalytic Study of the Child*, 36: 3–32.

Erna Furman (1992). *Toddlers and Their Mothers: A Study in Early Personality Development*. Madison, CT: International Universities Press.

Anna Freud, Humberto Nágera, and John Bolland also wrote *Anna Freud's Developmental Profile: Modifications and Present Form*. Available on the Carter-Jenkins Center website.

2. It is not that the contents of the reports were bad, but that the copies were of poor quality. They might have been mimeographed or carbon paper copies. Photocopy machines, a new technology at that time, were not so readily available in 1962.
3. I could not find this paper ("Diagnostic Skills and their Growth in Psycho-Analysis") under this title in Anna Freud's collected works, but it appears to be a first draft of what came to be the first section of "The Psychoanalytic View of Childhood: Long-Distance and Close-Up," in her 1965 book *Normality and Pathology in Childhood: Assessments of Development. The Writings of Anna Freud*, Vol. VI, pp. 3–24. New York: International Universities Press.
4. Nágera was leading a seminar at the Hampstead Clinic on Freud's libido theory.

DOCUMENT 13   ANNA FREUD, HUMBERTO NÁGERA and JOHN BOLLAND

Anna Freud, Humberto Nágera and John Bolland also wrote *Anna Freud's Developmental Profile: Modifications and Present Form*. They considered this article an on-going work in progress and so never published it. Nonetheless, Nágera made it available on the Carter-Jenkins Center website and the introduction is presented below. Numbered notes in the body of this next document and described at its end are from the original document and are not my annotations. D.B.

[Undated ongoing piece of work]

ANNA FREUD'S DEVELOPENTAL PROFILE:
Modifications and Present Form

Anna Freud, LL.D., Sc.D.
Humberto Nágera, M.D., B.Sc.
John Bolland, M.B., Ch.B.

This paper forms part of a Study entitled "Assessment of Pathology in Childhood," which was conducted at the Hampstead Child-Therapy Clinic, London in the 1960s. This investigation was supported in part by Public Health Service Research Grant, M-5683-0405, from the National Institute of Mental Health, Washington.

INTRODUCTION

The "Developmental Profile" outlined by Anna Freud in her paper "Assessment of Childhood Disturbances"(1) was applied and discussed at the Hampstead Child-Therapy Clinic for many years. This paper summarizes the modifications and developments in the Profile as it evolved over the years and follows on Dr. Nágera's paper "The Developmental Profile. Some Considerations Regarding its Clinical Application" (2).

Many staff members and students of the Child-Therapy Course have worked, as individuals and as members of groups, at this research, and we acknowledge our debt to them. The system of cross-membership of groups in the Clinic has meant that the central group working on the Developmental Profile, the Profile Research Group, has been able to collate material from all the other groups (3).

The general organization of the developmental profile remains unchanged, with one notable exception. This exception arose from the expansion of section V. C (Development of the Total Personality) by Anna Freud (4). As the Lines of Development were regarded as being on a different conceptual level from the other sections, they are now usually put as an appendix after section IX before the section on Diagnosis.

It is not surprising that the general organization has remained almost unaltered, as it was based on psychoanalytic assumptions and propositions which have been well tested through the years. Equally unsurprising was the finding that when the Profile was applied to clinical material of the most diverse nature, many questions were posed.

The questions fell into two broad categories, firstly, those concerning concepts which are not adequately understood; secondly, those arising when it was found that the Profile in its present form was inappropriate or inadequate to formulate a convincing picture of certain groups of disturbances.

In an attempt to answer questions in the first category, Study Groups were started to study particular theoretical problems, or groups already in existence were asked to undertake such work where it seemed appropriate.

The second category arose inevitably from our methodological approach. The Profile, while it aims ultimately at classifying the individual within a diagnostic schema, also aims at a more detailed examination of the "internal picture of the child which contains information about the *structure* of his personality; the *dynamic* interplay within the structure; some *economic* factors concerning drive activity and the relative strength of id and ego forces; his *adaptation* to reality; and some *genetic* assumptions." It was appreciated that the Profile was best suited for the study of the normal and neurotic personality. Nevertheless, we were also interested in the problems of assessing the development and disturbances of the blind, the "borderline" patient and the delinquent personality. Because we are at present largely ignorant of the intimate nature of such developmental problems and their relation to normal or neurotic development, we believed it to be methodologically sound to start studies on the basis of the basic Profile in each of these Groups. This approach has led to attempts to prepare Profile Drafts specific to each group. Some specially important hypotheses have been made about the blind and the borderline cases, and work is proceeding in the delinquent group. References are made in another paper to all these contributions (5).

In addition to these three groups, the Profile has also been adapted to meet the special problems of assessing the disturbances of later years. One adaptation was for the assessment of the adolescent personality and its psychopathology (6).

A Profile for the assessment of the adult personality was similarly prepared to facilitate comparative studies between children and parents (7).

Finally, modifications and amplifications have been found necessary in the preparation of the Terminal Profile (8). This is set up at the end of treatment. The modifications will be found under the appropriate sections below, but it should be noted that the aims of the Terminal Profile are as stated in "Assessment of Childhood Disturbances," i.e., "not only . . . the completion and verification of diagnosis but also . . . to measure treatment results . . ."

NOTES:

1. Freud, A. (1962). "Assessment of Childhood Disturbances." .*Psychoanalytic Study of the Child*. 17:149–158. And in *Writings of Anna Freud*, Vol. V, pp. 26–59.
2. Nágera, H. (1963). "The Developmental Profile, Considerations Regarding Its Clinical Application". *Psychoanalytic Study of the Child*, Vol. XVIII, New York, International Universities Press.
3. We are grateful to Dr. E. Koch and Miss P. Radford, whose Minutes of discussions in the Profile Research Group have proved invaluable in the preparation of this paper.
4. Freud, Anna, "The Concept of the Lines of Development," *The Psychoanalytic Study of the Child*, Vol. XVIII, 1963.
5. Nágera, H., and Bolland, J., "The Present Form of the Developmental Profile." Unpublished.
6. Laufer, M. (1965). "Assessment of Adolescent Disturbances: The Application of Anna Freud's Diagnostic Profile." *Psychoanalytic Study of the Child*. 20: 99–123.
7. Freud, A., Nágera, H., and Freud, W. E.: Metapsychological Assessment of the Adult Personality, *Psychoanalytic Study of the Child*, Vol. XX, New York, International Universities Press, 1965.

Also published in *The Writings of Anna Freud*, Vol. V, New York, International Universities Press, 1969.

8. The Terminal Profile is based on the whole treatment material, whereas the Diagnostic Profile is based only on the usual diagnostic investigations. The Terminal Profile should also note: a) the child's age at the beginning and end of treatment; b) the frequency of sessions and total duration of treatment; and the nature, frequency, etc. of the contact with the parents of the child.

DOCUMENT 14   ANNA FREUD

20 Maresfield Gardens
London

December 13, 1962

Dr. Humberto Nágera [1]
Hampstead Clinic
21 Maresfield Gardens
London N.W.3.

Dear Dr. Nágera,

To confirm our conversation of last week.

I am sorry that the case for you has not materialized so far. Our suggestion is that we should add to your salary what we would have paid for the case, namely £500 par annum and ask you to spend the equivalent time on the project work [2] in the Clinic. If an appropriate case should turn up in the future, please let us re-discuss the situation. Please confirm formally for our files whether this proposal meets with your wishes. We should like to begin the new agreement from 1st December 1962 from which time onward your salary would be £ 2000 per annum.

Yours sincerely,
Annafreud

1. Dr. Nágera's address listed here is 21 Maresfield Gardens, which was the Hampstead Clinic, directly across the street from Anna Freud's home.
2. "Project work" refers to all the research projects going on at the Clinic, which Nágera was increasingly involved with, if not leading.

DOCUMENT 15   ANNA FREUD

20 Maresfield Gardens
London

January 25, 1963

Dear Dr. Nágera,

We have revised our salaries again so that we now pay all analysts at the rate of two guineas [1] per hour (and not according to the Health Service scale as the Centenary Fund [2] has to do). This brings your yearly salary for your official 25 hours per week to £ 2,730 and we hope that you will be pleased with this increase. We hope it will be all right for you if this begins with January 1, 1963.

Yours sincerely,
Annafreud

1. A guinea is a British coin equivalent to 21 schillings. Before 1971, twenty schillings equaled one pound.
2. The Centenary Fund was money raised at the time of the Sigmund Freud Centennial Celebrations in May 1956. The monies were used to fund seminars and research.

DOCUMENT 16   ANNA FREUD

University Towers, Apt. 11
100 York Street, New Haven, Conn. [1]

April 1, 1963

Dear Dr. Nágera,

I saw Dr. Ruth Eissler [2] on Saturday evening and gave her your paper and she telephoned me yesterday to say that she likes it very much and that she is specially interested in your ideas about fixation and regression. I am very glad and she will confirm acceptance also directly to you.

Work begins today. I am already very curious.

Yours sincerely
Annafreud

1. The New Haven, Connecticut address gave Nágera the impression that Anna Freud was probably visiting with the Eisslers after lecturing in New Haven at Yale University, which she did on occasion.
2. Dr. Ruth Eissler (1906–1989) was a German psychiatrist who did her psychoanalytic training in Vienna in the 1930s. She married Dr. Kurt Eissler in 1936 and emigrated to New York, where she practiced psychoanalysis and was editor of *The Psychoanalytic Study of the Child*.

DOCUMENT 17   HEINZ HARTMANN

Heinz Hartmann M.D. [1]
1150 Fifth Avenue
New York City

July 15, 1963

Dear Dr. Nágera:

I want to thank you very much for letting me read the results of the work of your Concept Group [2] (only some parts of it had been known to me before). Your letter and the material came just in time for me to take them over the weekend to my country place—the only place where I have time for undisturbed reading.

I think that you and your group have done an exemplary job, outstanding through its thoroughness and clear-sightedness. Once it has been published, it will be of the greatest importance for every analyst on any level of education from the beginners to the most sophisticated. It will also greatly facilitate the work of Freud historians who will try to trace the history of individual concepts in Freud's work—when a concept was introduced, when a change of meaning took place, when it was superseded by others etc. For this too I find important prolegomena in your study. I hope that it will be soon made accessible to all of us.

As to content I have off hand only one comment to make. In your chapter on 'Conflict' I missed a reference to Freud's hypothesis on the impact of free aggression on conflict formation (in "Analysis Terminable and Interminable"). Few analysts have used it so far but I think it is an important idea and thus have made it the basis of a hypothesis of my own [2].

Thanking you once more,
Sincerely yours,
Heinz Hartmann, M.D.

1. Heinz Hartmann, M.D. (1894–1970) was a Viennese psychoanalyst who was analyzed by Sigmund Freud and became one of the leading proponents of ego psychology—the branch of psychoanalysis dedicated to Freud's structural model of the mind organized not only around the id, but around the id, ego, and superego. Ego psychology attends to the ego's normal and pathological development, the management of the impulses, and adaptation to reality. These are all themes very much at the forefront of Anna Freud's work as well. Hartmann was one of the ego psychology triumvirate of Hartmann, Kris, and Loewenstein.

2. The Concept Group was a Hampstead Clinic research project dedicated to studying, in scholarly detail, the historical development of Freud's most basic concepts pertaining to libido theory, dreams, instincts, metapsychology, conflicts, anxiety, and other subjects. With Nágera as the chairman, fifteen analysts and therapists worked intensively over six years and produced four published books on their findings. Nágera recalled, "I had much contact with Hartmann at International meetings and in correspondence. He was one of a number of distinguished analysts to whom I sent the Concept Group drafts for their revision and comments."

3. Hartmann refers to "the impact of free aggression on conflict formation." This is probably in reference to Hartmann's theoretical proposition, of the process of neutralization, which was described by Blanck and Blanck (1974). The process of neutralization "moves both libidinal and aggressive energies from the instinctual to the noninstinctual mode, thereby rendering them available to the ego. Noting that Freud's proposals about sublimation preceded his dual drive theory, it seemed logical to Hartmann to enlarge the concept of sublimation by including within consideration of drive-taming processes the vicissitudes of the aggressive drive. . . . The capacity to neutralize drive energy, working in a circular, expanding interaction with the capacity to delay drive discharge, places energies for ego building (structuralization) and expanding ego functions at the disposal of the infant." (Blanck & Blanck, 1974, pp. 33–34)

DOCUMENT 18   RALPH R. GREENSON

Ralph R. Greenson M.D. [1]
436 North Roxbury Drive
Beverly Hills, California

July 21, 1963

Dear Dr. Nágera:

I want to thank you very much for the material you sent me on the concept research material. I have already read parts of it and find it extremely useful. I think it is enormously worthwhile to have the basic concepts available with particular emphasis on the historical development of Freud's ideas. It is very useful in teaching. For example, I have to give some lectures to medical students on Freud's Instinct Theory in September, and find the chapters on aggression, death instinct, auto-eroticism, narcissism, component instincts, very valuable. It is not only clearly written but it saves me an enormous amount of time to trace these things out for myself. I wish I had the other chapters which deal with other aspects of his instinct theory.

I want to thank you and the members of your group for sending me this material.

Sincerely yours,
Ralph R. Greenson, M.D.

1. Ralph R. Greenson, M.D. (1911–1979) was a prominent American psychiatrist and psychoanalyst who was analyzed by Otto Fenichel and belonged to the ego psychology tradition in the U.S. His book, *The Technique and Practice of Psychoanalysis* (1967), was a classic text on psychoanalytic technique for many years. He was well known as the analyst and friend of many Hollywood stars and was also a close friend of Anna Freud. Nágera had some contact with Greenson through the years and he sought out Greenson's feedback on the early drafts of the Concept Group's work.

DOCUMENT 19   ANNA FREUD

Far End
Walberswick

August 17, 1963

Dear Dr. Nágera,

Enclosed is the letter from the Foundations' Fund. May I have it back, please, for the files and also for Dr. Eissler after you have read it?

I have answered in your and my name that we withdraw the application and that we shall submit a different one. I have also said that for our own use we do not make such a difference between empirical and scholastic studies since we find conceptualization such an indispensable tool in clinical investigation.

But, never mind! The money comes from elsewhere at the moment and new sources will open.

Best regards,
yours sincerely
Annafreud

DOCUMENT 20   ANNA FREUD

Far End
Walberswick

September 8, 1963

Dear Dr. Nágera,

I was very glad to have your letter and enclosures. I think the paper is most interesting and I put my remarks concerning it on a separate sheet.

Now to your questions:

1) Washington [1]: I shall be in the Clinic on Wednesday, 11th September, 2–4 p.m. for an Administrative Meeting since I pass through London on that day. I shall know then whether any forms from the N.I.M.H. have arrived and we can settle the details. By the way: please look once more at the copy of my Developmental Lines [2]. There is a mistake in the numbering of pages, p. 16 missing in the numbers (no text missing). This can be corrected easily.

2) James [3]: very interesting I wonder: would not irregular appointments, when needed by him, [be] better than fixed weekly ones which usually yield very little?

3) Wednesday meetings: I should like to leave decision about starting to you.

About the program: we should discuss this so that it coincides somewhat with the points of the next Washington report.

4) I return Helen Ross' [4] letter which is very nice.

5) I am very curious about the beginning work of the Clinical Research Group.

See you on Wednesday!

Yours sincerely
Annafreud

1. "Washington" refers to the location of the National Institute of Mental Health where Miss Freud and Dr. Nágera were seeking research grants.
2. Developmental Lines: See "The Concept of Developmental Lines" in Anna Freud (1965). *Normality and Pathology in Childhood: Assessments of Development: The Writings of Anna Freud*, Vol. VI, pp. 62–92. New York: International Universities Press.
3. Pseudonym
4. Helen Ross (1890–1978) was an American psychoanalyst who was analyzed by Helene Deutsch in Vienna. She became a close friend of Anna Freud and was instrumental in securing funding for the Hampstead Clinic through the Marshall Field Foundation in Chicago.

DOCUMENT 21   EMANUEL WINDHOLZ

Emanuel Windholz, M.D. [1]
2420 Sutter St.
San Francisco

November 26, 1963

Dear Doctor Nágera,

It is very impressive to read the work of the Concept Research Group. It is an overwhelming task and yet it could not be substituted by any other approach.

The usefulness of this contribution is manifold. It will remove the confusion which arises from the incorrect use of concepts. Above all, it will facilitate understanding of many aspects of Freud's work. It will force the students to recognize the fact that many of his formulations were changed, and an understanding of these changes will increase our insight into those areas of psychoanalysis which required preliminary concepts. Without these Freud could have lost sight of many facts which he gradually understood.

The limitations of your work are obvious. Others will be encouraged to carry it further by extending the same approach to a research of concepts of others who have carried on Freud's work, and are indispensable for our understanding of the present status of psychoanalysis.

I am most appreciative of your willingness to share with us your unpublished papers and I hope you may be willing to send me additional material.

Sincerely yours,
Emanuel Windholz M.D.

1. Emanuel Windholz, M.D. (1903–1986) was a Czechoslovakian psychoanalyst who had been analyzed by Moshe Wulff, Otto Fenichel and Frances Deri. He was on the organizing committee that placed the commemorative plaque on Freud's birth house in Pribor, Czechoslovakia in 1931 in honor of Freud's 75th birthday. He immigrated to San Francisco

before the Second World War and took a leading role in establishing, in 1942, the San Francisco Psychoanalytic Society (now the San Francisco Center for Psychoanalysis), under the guidelines of the American Psychoanalytic Association.

DOCUMENT 22   ANNA FREUD

Far End
Walberswick

January 2, 1964

Dear Dr. Nágera,

I am working hard on my book [1] and re-reading what I wrote last year. I have just discovered that you were right in our last discussion when you said I had written about regression versus arrest concerning the obsessional neurosis [2] and I could not remember it. I came upon the passage by chance and copied it out for you. (Enclosed.) The trouble with me is that there are such long intervals in my writing that I forget what is past and concentrate on the present.

But that is not the real reason for this letter. More important to me I have now finished the 2 sections which I am going to read to the Clinic on 2 Wednesdays, namely on <u>Homosexuality</u>, and on the <u>Perversions</u>, both as diagnostic categories applied to the assessment of childhood disorders. I would very much like to check them with you before reading them to the Clinic as I did with the <u>Delinquency</u> section [3]. But this time I have no typed copy, which means no copy at all, only the handwritten original from which I do not like to part. Do you think you could stand having it read out to you after I come back?

Yours sincerely
Annafreud

[Enclosed.]
Extract from Chapter IV
Section <u>Assessment by Development and its Implications</u> " - - - - I believe that there are several useful points for diagnosis which emerge from this closer scrutiny of the child's normal developmental processes.

a) <u>The Results of Imbalance between Id and Ego</u>

There are, for one, the consequences of an uneven progression rate in drive-development on the one hand and ego- and superego-development on the other hand, which so far have been applied only to one particular instance, namely the formation of the obsessional neurosis.

For many years, the defense activity which produces obsessional symptoms has been known to be set in motion where a relatively highly developed ego, (including moral and aesthetic superego demands) finds itself confronted by drive components of a relatively lower order, via the anal-sadistic ones. Although in the etiology of the neuroses, this state of affairs is produced usually secondarily by regression of the drives, it can come about also primarily as the result of an environmentally or constitutionally determined precocious ego-development.

There is every reason to assume that the consequences of such imbalance can be explored further, for instance with regard to the opposite constellation where drive-development proceeds smoothly or with acceleration while ego- and superego-growth lags behind for whatever reasons - - - -"

1. The book Anna Freud is referring to here is *Normality and Pathology in Childhood: Assessments of Development, The Writings of Anna Freud*, Vol. VI, New York: International Universities Press. It is an organized presentation of more than forty years of research on child development. She addressed the various types of material for observation—derivatives of the unconscious, defense mechanisms, child behavior, and the ego—and described the similarities and differences between child and adult analyses. As previously mentioned, she introduced the concept of developmental lines, from dependence to emotional self-reliance and adult object relatedness;

from suckling to rational eating; from wetting and soiling to bladder and bowel control; from irresponsibility to responsibility in body management; from egocentricity to companionship; from body to toy; and from play to work. The developmental lines are normative paths around which one assesses the psychological structure and functioning of a child in order to understand pathology and to plan treatment. On the one hand, she described conflict-based neurotic disorders; on the other, arrests, defects, and deficiencies of development. The conflict-based neurotic disorders include (1) current behavioral disturbances occurring within a healthy range of normal variation, (2) symptoms arising from developmental strain, (3) permanent drive regressions leading to neurotic conflicts and character disorders, and (4) drive regressions along with ego and superego regressions leading to infantilism, borderline, delinquent, or psychotic disturbances. The arrests, defects, and deficiencies of development pertain to (1) deficiencies of an organic nature, or early deprivations that produce retarded, defective, and non-typical personalities, and (2) destructive processes of organic, toxic, or psychic origin that disrupt mental growth. Anna Freud's multidimensional approach to personality assessment helps us to see that the same symptom in different children may be derived from different sources: internal conflicts and deficits; external conflicts, deficits, and disturbances; and problems of organic and toxic origin. The therapeutic elements of a child analysis will depend on the assessment. Thus, not all children receive the same type of analysis. *Normality and Pathology in Childhood: Assessments of Development* (1965) is a book that is seen as a major contribution to psychoanalysis, equal in importance to *The Ego and the Mechanisms of Defense* (Dyer, 1983, p. 230).
2. Humberto Nágera had a growing interest in the obsessional neurosis at that time and Anna Freud shared in that interest. Nágera recalled, "We used to see children at Hampstead that showed obsessional behaviors already in the toddler stage that generally disappeared, in most cases, in the next phase, and we saw this in many other stages as well. I felt the need to determine what was an indication of obsessional neurosis or potential for it and what was not, etc."

3. Anna Freud addresses homosexuality, perversions, delinquency and more in Assessment of Pathology. Part II. Some infantile Prestages of Adult Psychopathology, in *Normality and Pathology in Childhood: Assessments of Development* (1965), *The Writings of Anna Freud*, Vol. VI, pp. 148–212, New York: International Universities Press.

DOCUMENT 23   ANNA FREUD

20 Maresfield Gardens
London

January 26, 1964

Dear Dr. Nágera,

I am quite impressed with our adult Profile [1]. It looks much more complete than I had expected and I think we should continue with it before other people take it out of our hands. Did I tell you that last year in New Haven I used such a profile tentatively in a discussion with the Training Committee of the Western New England Society and even before the alterations, they found it very useful.

There are several improvements which we can make still:

1) The various manifestations of adult sex life can be made more explicit even where they are additions and introductions to normal intercourse. My discussion in New Haven was about the point that they tried to assess the personality of a candidate without having a clue to their sex life [2].

2) Attitude to money has to be stressed even more. Also details about attitudes to co-workers, superiors and subordinates.

3) <u>Stealing</u> and <u>lying</u> which are such good common symptoms with children are not the right examples for adults. We have to find different ones of multiple causation.

It will be easy to make the alterations when we apply it to cases.

Yours sincerely
Annafreud

1. The reference to the Adult Profile was an article Dr. Nágera was writing. It was based on Anna Freud's teachings, and was being worked out in a small team composed of Anna Freud, Humberto Nágera, and W. Ernest Freud (Anna Freud's nephew and the only Freud grandchild to become a psychoanalyst). Dr. Nágera recalled, "I wrote the actual paper but it was based on concepts that Anna Freud had developed and that I was very familiar with. I had heard her through the years expound on them and at some point I decided to put it together in this form, so that other people could enjoy the knowledge that she had condensed on the Diagnostic Profile. And so I wrote it, but I put her name as the first author because the concepts, for the most part were hers. There might be some that were mine but the large majority of it was Anna Freud. And, of course, Ernest was very interested in this and he was very close to me, he was also very close to Anna Freud. He was interested in the Profile and later wrote the Baby Profile and so he wanted to participate and he did. But he helped me with some material and so I made him the third author. The three of us met together on two or three different occasions. I circulated the draft and then we got together and discussed it—Anna Freud, Ernest and I. And then we arrived to the final formulations that got published." Their completed article was published the following year. Freud, A., Nágera, H., & Freud, W. E. (1965/1969). Metapsychological assessment of the adult personality: The adult profile. *Psychoanalytic Study of the Child*, 20:9–41. And in *Writings of Anna Freud*, Vol. V, 60–75.
2. I asked Dr. Nágera what Anna Freud might be looking for in the sexual life of a psychoanalytic candidate and what implications it might have for the candidate's suitability for training. Nágera replied: "Had the candidate reached adult sexual maturity? Or did the candidate have significant fixations in some of the earlier stages of psychosexual

development? Without such an assessment you really cannot be sure of the nature of their conflicts, analyzability, etc."

―ⁿⁿ―

DOCUMENT 24   SANDOR LORAND

Sandor Lorand M.D. [1]
40 West 59th Street
New York 19, New York

January 29, 1964

Dear Dr. Nágera,

I am sorry to be so delayed in thanking you for the material concerning the work of the Concept Research Group of the Hampstead Clinic. I appreciate your generous gesture in letting me have the study and to learn of the excellent work your group is doing. I had many months to study it—to read and re-read the material. You and your co-workers certainly have covered a great deal in this excellent study.

The systematic study of material presented, the theoretical assumptions, and observations are all very clearly stated. The follow-up study and the investigation of the various constructions are well thought out and carefully executed and most lucidly presented. The study is timely because at present theories and new formulations by various analysts on the same concept are so divergent. (See for instance the studies of object relationship.) The material is most stimulating and will be of interest to every analyst.

The presentation conveys in a simple, clear manner the complexity of the concepts. The overall information which it provides will make it an important source of knowledge about psychoanalytic theory and psychoanalysis as a science. It will be important to all analysts, especially to those in training.

Yours sincerely,
Sandor Lorand, M.D.

P.S. On another occasion I will write you about your paper "Developmental Profile".

1. Sandor Lorand, M.D. (1893–1987) was a Hungarian psychiatrist and psychoanalyst who was analyzed by Sandor Ferenczi. After emigrating to the United States he settled in New York, where he was recognized as a distinguished psychoanalyst who not only practiced, but taught and wrote extensively.

DOCUMENT 25   DOROTHY BURLINGHAM

20 Maresfield Gardens
London

February 13, 1964

Dear Dr. Nágera,

I am impressed with your paper on the blind [1] and your formulation. I was especially interested in the part on verbalization.

There are several parts I should like to discuss with you, after I have read it far more carefully.

I believe that a lot of this backwardness would fall away with better understanding of what the blind child needs in the first year of life. I think there are different types of backwardness caused by quite different reasons, only one of which is the lack of sight. And this false backwardness is of apparent backwardness, the egos of the blind work well on their different aims.

From my experience and reading I think the adult blind is not as you picture him but I may have misunderstood what you mean.

I am so glad that you became interested in the blind. What a lot you have <u>added</u> to our work. I certainly am grateful.

Yours sincerely
Dorothy Burlingham [2]

1. Nágera's paper opens with the following paragraph: "This study is based on six blind children observed in our Unit for the Blind. It is an attempt to organize and describe by means of Profile headings what was learned during "periods of observation," analytic treatment, and diagnostic profiles about this group of children. For each of the children a developmental profile was prepared and discussed in the "Profile Research Group at the Hampstead Clinic" (Humberto Nágera, 1981). "The Contribution of Sight to Ego and Drive Development" can be found in Nágera's *The Developmental Approach to Child Psychopathology* (1981), pp. 231–246 and 247–267.
2. Dorothy Tiffany Burlingham (1891–1979) was the granddaughter of the famous jewelry artist, Charles Lewis Tiffany, and the daughter of the famous glass artist, Louis Comfort Tiffany. She married Dr. Robert Burlingham and had four children with him: Bob, Mabbie, Tinky and Mikey. But soon Dr. Burlingham developed a severe bipolar affective disorder and her children started demonstrating problems of their own. Dorothy needed to get away from her husband if only to save her children from the chaos of their father's manic rages and crushing depressions. She moved to Vienna in 1925 and went into analysis, first with Theodore Reik and then with Sigmund Freud. All four of her children entered analysis with Anna Freud and soon Dorothy Burlingham, Anna Freud and Eva Rosenfeld joined forces to establish a private school (The Hietzing School) where they employed a couple of young teachers, Peter Blos and Erik Erikson. Dorothy Burlingham went through psychoanalytic training, became an analyst, and became Anna Freud's closest friend and confidant. In the 1930s Dorothy and her children lived upstairs from the Freuds at Berggasse 19 and in London Dorothy shared the Freud home at 20 Maresfield Gardens.

Anna Freud and Dorothy Burlingham were the closest of friends and colleagues and remained so for the rest of their lives, working together in their Hietzing School and Jackson Nursery in Vienna and then in England, working first in their war nurseries and then in the Hampstead Clinic.

DOCUMENT 26   ANNA FREUD

Far End
Walberswick

February 16, 1964

Dear Dr. Nágera,

I looked for you in the Clinic on Thursday but I missed you. I just wanted to say how much I like your paper and that I think your discussion of the various points is quite brilliant and very convincing. It all comes over very well, the differences in drive and ego development and above all the danger of reading into the processes of the blind our preconceptions taken from the study of the seeing.

There is only one point which worries me a bit and which I would like to discuss with you still if you want to: That is the extent of legitimate generalization which varies somewhat throughout the paper. What I have in mind is the following: There are many points which refer to all people born blind as such and have doubtless the widest general application; but there are also others which may refer only to the children studied and others like them and might not be applicable to the very intelligent blind (of which Mike and Ron are examples), whose ego-processes seem to be more like in the seeing. (Why? Do they merely compensate earlier? And does this greater similarity concern only the ego, not the drives and object relations?)

Anyway, I wonder whether it would not be possible to distinguish in some way between these 2 types of data (those with general and those with restricted application) perhaps it means no more than that the very intelligent blind arrive earlier than the others at the point which you describe on page 20 and which we have not yet been able to study in analysis.

On Thursday afternoon Alice Goldberger [1] gave a fascinating description of her blind Jane who evidently has not yet taken possession of her own body, except in music, on the piano, when she is suddenly in control of her hands. It would have interested you very much.

(Do you think that, possibly, learning Braille and reading has something to do with the belated ego-advance? But that may be nonsense.)

Yours sincerely
Annafreud

1. Alice Goldberger (1897–1986) was a German-Jewish youth instructor who opened up a shelter for disadvantaged children in pre-war Germany, but when Hitler came to power she had to shut it down and flee to England. As a German in England at war with Germany, she was interned for a time on the Isle of Man as a "Friendly Enemy Alien." In the internment camp she opened up a children's facility. Anna Freud heard about her work and, after Alice Goldberger was freed from internment, invited her to come work with her at the War Nurseries, which she did. After the war England opened its doors to 732 war orphans who were survivors of the concentration camps. Twenty-eight houses were set up to care for them and Alice Goldberger was in charge of one of them—Weir Courtney, outside of London. The house was in operation from 1945–1957 and closed down only after all the children had either been adopted or grew old enough to head out on their own. Miss Goldberger never had children of her own but stayed in touch with these foster-children throughout the years. See Bateson, J. (2010). *The Holocaust Survivors at Weir Courtney, Lingfield*. The RH7 History Group. http://www.rh7.org/factshts/holocst.pdf (accessed September 13, 2013). Nágera recalled: "Alice Goldberger was a very nice, modest, Jewish lady who managed to escape from the Nazis to England, promising her family that once in England she would get them out of Nazi Germany. She tried but was not successful and her whole family was exterminated. She worked with Anna when they were bringing orphan Jewish

children to England. She followed them all through her whole life, and went to their marriages, etc. in whatever country they may have emigrated to. She was a mother to all of them and was very much loved by them. The BBC had a program entitled *This is Your Life*, and one show was dedicated to her, and many of these children came to England to be with her on that program. Alice was a lovable human being."

DOCUMENT 27   ANNA FREUD

20 Maresfield Gardens
London

June 19, 1964

Dear Dr. Nágera,

I think you will enjoy reading this [1].

Yours sincerely
Annafreud

1. "This" refers to the following research proposal for the Concept Group, which had already begun its work and had funding but was perhaps seeking additional funding. "Point 1" is missing, so we don't know to whom the proposal was addressed. The proposal is eighteen pages long—some handwritten by Miss Freud, others typed and two sections handwritten by Dr. Nágera. It is a very rough draft with arrows and instructions from this page to that. I have done my best to piece it together as well as I could.

POINT 2
A) <u>Principal Investigator</u>: Dr. Humberto Nágera

B) <u>Permanent consultant</u> Anna Freud LL.D.

C) <u>Other research participants:</u>

Miss Baker, Mr. Holder, Mrs. Neurath, Miss Putzel, Miss Radford, Mr. Laufer, Mr. Meers, Miss Colonna, Miss First, Miss Rees, Miss Edgcumbe, Mrs. Gavshon, Miss Jones, Mrs. Dansky, Mr. Koch, Mrs. Burgner, Miss Hodgson, Mrs. Weitzner

a) Qualified psycho-analysts and graduates of the Hampstead Child Therapy Course

b) Students of the Hampstead Child Therapy Course

POINT 3

CENTRAL RESEARCH IDEA:

Scholastic Research Work on basic psychoanalytic concepts beginning with Freud's postulations and the development of psychoanalytic theory throughout his works.

At a later stage it is planned to move to psychoanalytic literature in general, so as to include other authors as well, at least so far as a limited number of truly basic concepts are concerned. This material will be published and made available to people in the psychoanalytic and related fields who can approach with the help of the concepts any point in the development of a given theory in which they may have particular interest or perhaps follow its historical growth and its interaction with related aspects. The working group is referred to in what follows by the abbreviated title of "Concept Group."

AIMS:

The work of the Concept Group is carried out within the frame-work of the studies of the Hampstead Child-Therapy Course and Clinic in close connection with the departments for research, training, diagnosis, and therapy to which it gives service in the following ways:

a) Service to the Index Department

One of the central projects of our clinic is the Hampstead Index of Analytic Material which is concerned with the classification of our clinical material into meaningful small units. (This project has been assisted by grants from the Foundation's Fund from 1954 to 1963 and progress reports as well as samples of its work have been sent regularly to the Foundation's Fund during this period.) This work has highlighted the necessity of having clear-cut and more precise theoretical formulations to encompass the case material. Since many basic psychoanalytic concepts have had a long historic development and were formulated in different terms at different times, much confusion is bound to arise and the need is clear for precise formulations. These formulations must be comprehensive and take into account the development of any given concept, as well as its relationship to the rest of the theory.

b) Service to the project "Assessment of Pathology in Childhood"

Another important project of the Hampstead Clinic is an improvement of diagnostic thinking by means of a developmental picture or "profile" of the child, a study financed at present by the National Institute of Mental Health, Washington. The formulation of these assessments depend for their meaningfullness on the precision of conceptual thinking and many queries are thrown up by them which are referred for clarification to the Concept Group. Similar needs are naturally emerging all the time from the various other research projects [unclear].

c) Service to Students and Teachers and Authors in Psychoanalysis

Students doing their psychoanalytic training will have in a condensed but meaningful way an encyclopaedic review of basic concepts in psychoanalysis. From it they can readily refer to Freud's work in order to pursue and become fully acquainted with his formulations. In this way they can either study specific aspects or get a more comprehensive and over-all look at any given subject.

Some lecturers and seminar leaders at the Hampstead Clinic have used some of these concepts as the basic ground for their lectures or seminars. They have, so far, got a good response from the students. At the same time, they have found the concepts an economic device for the preparation of lectures or seminars where otherwise very many hours of work would have been required.

Analysts, suffering as they do from a marked limitation of time may welcome the availability of the concepts, when they are in the process of writing papers on subjects of their interest or clinical experience. The otherwise necessary and prolonged labor of reading the relevant bibliography in Freud is thus reduced to a minimum.

Altogether the work may help to avoid confusion and constantly reformulations and introductions of new terms, to refer to concepts already clearly described by Freud in the past.

[Next paragraph by Dr. Nágera]

The concepts thus arrived at are used by the Clinical Concept Research Group and the Index Department. In some cases the concepts will fit their essential needs for classification and study of their clinical material. In others the clinical material will reveal the need for further conceptual formulations in specific problematic or insufficiently studied areas. This further study will be carried out by the personnel concerned in these departments while the Concept Group continues it scholastic researches.

[End of Nágera paragraph.]

METHODS

The Concept Group consists at present of a number of qualified psychoanalysts and analytic child-therapists plus the junior and senior students of the Hampstead Child Therapy Course.

The group tries to follow the historical development of the concepts, noting the changes that take place as the theory develops, and the influence which such developments may have on related subjects etc.

Work was started by approaching in this way the "Theory of Dreams", trying to study a number of essential concepts underlying it. This was followed by work moving to psychoanalytic formulations relating to "The Libido Theory" and "The Theory of Instincts."

The work is carried out in the following way: A given psychoanalytic concept is assigned to each member of the Group. It is this person's task to look all through Freud's published papers, books, correspondence, minutes of the Vienna Psycho-Analytic Society, etc. for the relevant material in order to present it in two or three months' time to the Group in what we call the "Personal Draft" stage of the concept.

In this draft and whenever appropriate, literal quotations from Freud are used. This "Personal Draft" is then circulated among the members of the Group some time before it is due for discussion so that it can be studied thoroughly. It is then discussed at a meeting of the whole Group and out of this discussion a "Group Draft" is produced.

The "Group Draft" is expected to be a stage more advanced and organized than the "Personal Draft."

The final draft is settled by an editorial committee from the Group so as to achieve uniformity of style.

Work Completed So Far:

So far group drafts have been finalized on ----- concepts and sent for their comments to an International Advisory Committee consisting of senior leading members of the International Psychoanalytical Association especially from the American Psychoanalytic Association. A list of these concepts as well as samples selected from them are attached.

Point 4

Budget Estimate:

Our budget is based on the expectation that the Principal Investigator plus the other research participants will give approximately 8 hours per week to the project. Salaries for qualified psychoanalysts are calculated on the basis of 2–3 pounds per hour, for qualified child-therapists on the basis of 1–2 pounds per hour (depending on seniority). Students work on the scheme on the basis of Training Grants supplied from other sources. The scheme would further demand the services of one senior and one junior shorthand-typist (together approximately £1000 per year). Altogether the expenses for professional salaries and secretaries wages would come to approximately 5000 £ = $15,000 per year excluding overheads (Approximately 3000 professional working hours)

POINT 5

OTHER SOURCES OF SUPPORT

At the present moment the whole program of the Hampstead Child Therapy Clinic is supported by the following Foundations.

The Field Foundation, Inc. New York (for the purposes of clinical work)

The Grant Foundation, Inc. New York (for educational and medical services)

The Psychoanalytic Research and Development Fund (for theoretical and clinical investigation)

The Taconic Foundation, New York (for clinical purposes)

The Old Dominion Foundation, U.S.A. (for Students' Grants)

The National Institute of Mental Health US Department of Health, Education and Welfare for the project "Assessment of Pathology in Childhood".

POINT 6

BRIEF STATEMENT OF FACILITIES:

The facilities available are (a) man-power, (b) reference material and (c) premises.

(a) There is a readily available pool of trained analysts and child-therapists who are interested in the theoretical aspects of their work, together with students (already trained in other disciplines and familiar with psychological research techniques) who are at various stages of their analytic child-therapy training. This large group does the basic reading research.

(b) Reference material includes a good, and improving, library of psychoanalytic literature which is supplemented as necessary from the personal library of Miss Anna Freud. The Hampstead Index is available for reference to clinical material which may clarify the theoretical formulations being prepared.

(c) The premises of the Hampstead Child Therapy Clinic are available and serve as the physical backgrounds and setting for the Group.
Statement of facilities being done by Dr. Bolland.
16th July, 1963

Point 7

Curriculum Vitaes
For Miss Weiss to deal with
[written by Dr. Nágera]
Name: Anna Freud
Address: ----------------
Date of birth: 3/12/1895
Birthplace: Vienna
Present nationality: British
Degree: LL.D., h.c. Clark University Worchester Mass 1950

b) Other research training etc.:

1) Psychoanalytic Institute Vienna-London Psychoanalyst and Training Analyst 1925 -----

2) Hampstead Nurseries London Child Development 1940–45

3) Hampstead Child Therapy Course and Clinic London, Child Development 1947

[End of Dr. Nágera paragraph]

POINT 8

LIST OF PUBLICATIONS

There are so far no publications from this project (publications from members of the Hampstead Child Therapy Course and Clinic have been sent regularly to the Foundations and under the terms of our former grants).

DOCUMENT 28   ANNA FREUD

20 Maresfield Gardens
London

July 12, 1964

Dear Dr. Nágera,

I have just read the interesting minutes of the Concept Research Group Meeting, 5th of June on "Thinking". This brings me to a question:

You have heard Mark Thompsen's [1] discussion remarks the other day, suggesting that the child acquires secondary process thinking in imitation of the mother. I did not answer but to me this seems all wrong and reducing a process of ego maturation to an adjunct of object relationship. But I would like very much to have your opinion on it.

Yours sincerely
Annafreud

1. Pseudonym.

DOCUMENT 29   ANNA FREUD

London

July 22, 1964

Mr. Philip Sapir
Chief,
Research Grants and Fellowships Branch
National Institute of Mental Health
Department of Health, Education and Welfare
National Bank Building
Bethesda 14, Maryland

Dear Mr. Sapir,

My co-workers and I have pleasure in sending you, under separate cover, the Progress Report concerning the <u>second</u> year of grant (MH–05683–02) for our project "Assessment of Pathology in Childhood".

As in the previous year, contributions to the investigations carried out by means of and within the frame-work of the "Profile" itself, were made by all the departments of our organization, in cooperation and interchange with the specially set up Profile Research Committee. This gave rise to a series of clinical and theoretical papers which are enclosed in the Report, together with samples of the studies which led up to them. As indicated in the Table of Contents the papers produced during the current year as the direct or indirect outcome of Profile Studies number 12. Added to last year's production of 6 papers, this brings our list of publications under the grant to 18 up to the present date.

While in the first year of work, our assessments of pathology remained largely within the range from the near-normal to the severely neurotic children, the investigations of the current year were carried beyond the neuroses to the handicapped, the borderline, the traumatized, the infantile pre-stages of perversion and delinquency, as well as to specific factors affecting ego-development and it's arrests. The numerous questions opened up during these studies, as well as the adaptations of the profile itself when applied to different diagnostic categories and different age-groups require a substantial amount of further work.

We shall be glad to know whether this form of reporting meets with your requirements or whether you would like us to make any substantial changes or additions in next year's report.

Yours sincerely
Annafreud LL.D., Sc.D.

[NOTE: The following enclosed research proposal is incomplete, but elaborates on Anna Freud's thinking about the importance of working out the Adult Profile as a natural extension of the work on "The Assessment of Pathology in Childhood."]

Introduction

The need for a Profile of adult patients has made itself felt in our clinical work for some time already, especially for those cases where children and one or the other parent are in treatment simultaneously [1].

Our original profile schema was devised for neurotic child patients to facilitate the organization, under psychoanalytically meaningful sections, of material available about them (before, during or after therapy). Where subsequently the profile was applied beyond the scope of the neuroses, a number of sections had to be amplified and intensified to embrace all the details relevant for the individual's specific pathology. In the case of the Blind this concerned above all the headings concerned with phase development, fixation and regression; in the case of the Borderline children so far the sections containing information about Cathexis of Self and Cathexis of Objects were provided with sub-divisions to trace in more minute detail the locations of pathology. When applied to the characterization of the adolescent the profile schema had to be widened to accommodate the variations of superego development, ideal formation, and the identity problems which form an essential part of the adolescent's upheaval.

While the profile schema as such profited from these expansions and gained so far as it's scope of application was concerned the basic rationale underlying it remained untouched. For all the categories of disturbance enumerated above, assessment by profile remained on the basis of developmental considerations i.e. the individual was examined for his position on the progression sequences relevant to drive development, ego and superego development and the age-adequate developments of internal structuralization and adaptation to the environment respectively. Pathology was evaluated in all instances according to its interference with orderly and steady progress in these respects.

This basic rationale changes with the application of the profile scheme to the adult personality. What assessment is concerned with in this instance is not an ongoing process but a finished product in which by implication the ultimate developmental stages should have been reached. The developmental point of view may be upheld only in so far as success or failure to reach this level or to maintain themselves on it decides on the so-called maturity or maturation of the adult personality. For the rest, normality is judged by the quality of functioning (in sex, work and their sublimations) the pleasure in life derived from it and by the quality of the individual's object and community relationships. Pathology reveals itself through permanent symptomatology which interferes with any of the above aims by suffering for internal causes and/or by the individual's incapacity to relate realistically to his environment.

Since childhood and adult profiles are not identical in orientation, comparison between such assessments of parent and child will have to be restricted to the sections which come closest to each other. Still the schemas may prove invaluable for the correlation of items such as the importance within the [illegible] structure of the particular drives, the quality of the defense organization, the content of ideal self and super-ego, the developmental phase governing the quality of object relationships, etc.

Perversions as a diagnostic category in the assessment of childhood disorders. (Addiction Transvestism, Fetishism.)

In recent years, child analysts have advanced considerably in their understanding of normal and abnormal child psychopathology and have shown themselves skilled increasingly in applying their knowledge to the upbringing of children and to their therapy. But compared with this adventurous spirit shown with regard to technique and theory, they have remained fairly conservative in another area of their work. So far as the classification of childhood disorders is concerned, they have been content mostly to take over the diagnostic categories as they were handed down to child psychiatry and child analysis not only from the field of adult analysis but also from adult psychiatry and criminology. These classifications do not serve the needs of the child analyst for a variety of reasons: some of them because they are descriptive; others because they are dynamic only while failing to accommodate the structural and adaptive aspects of the case; the majority because they neglect the developmental, i.e. genetic point of view on which the child analyst's thinking should be based.

These shortcomings of the diagnostic classification, as they are in current use, have been discussed before with regard to Dissociality, Criminality and Homosexuality. See two papers by the same author, "Dissociality, Delinquency, Criminality as Diagnostic Categories in the Assessment of Childhood Disorders" and "Homosexuality as a Diagnostic Category in the Assessment of Childhood Disorders". They become all the more conspicuous in the area of the perversions proper, a diagnostic term which cannot or should not be used outright in the children's field.

The reason for this is of course an obvious one. Since...
[NOTE: The rest of the document is missing]

1. Nágera recalled some aspects of the clinical work at the Hampstead Clinic, which further elaborate our view of the work being done there: "The Hampstead Clinic had quite a large number of rooms in which children would be seen and each of these rooms had in them some small cupboards with keys. And any room would have 10 maybe 15

cupboards and each cupboard contained the toys that you had chosen for that particular child. The toys depended on the age of the child and the interests that the child had, which you found out about through information obtained from the parents. What does he like? What does he play with? And you took a good look at what kind of problem the child was having—the main conflicts at that particular point in time. And consequently you try to combine all these things to choose the kind of toy that will lend itself to looking at that particular problem. And there were toys, of course, that you avoid like the plague because they don't lead anywhere. They are just used as resistances.

"So you choose the toys that you think will lend themselves particularly well for the child to express derivatives in play, using toys similar to what he liked to play with or relate to so that his interest could be developed that way. You chose those and usually you didn't have a lot of toys. You have maybe four or five toys in the cupboard and you always have some pencils, crayons, papers, plasticine and things like that. Some rooms had access to water but not all rooms. So the number of toys and the reason for the cupboard was that, let's say that he was building something with modeling clay or Legos. It is important that whatever he built was not destroyed by the next child that came in. In this way, he had his cupboard. When he came in, you gave him the key and he opened it and he does whatever he likes and nobody would interfere or destroy the toys or play with them. They were specific to that particular child and it had an enormous advantage that the child had a place of his own. Frequently they had siblings that were constantly messing with each other's toys and creating problems that way. And this way that personal cupboard of toys helped to build a relationship with the child that had a certain uniqueness to it. So that's the way the Clinic did it.

"Children, as you know, particularly young children, are completely unable to free associate. Catastrophic things may be happening at home and they may not be able to recount that to you, at all. They may not even have the cognitive ability to put that into words in a meaningful manner to you. But they'd be affected by it and they would express that in the play in the form of derivatives and so you had to decipher from the play what was going on with little ones. That was sometimes very difficult because as I said the sky may be falling down in the house but he wouldn't be able to verbalize that to you. So that you had regular meetings with the parents, particularly when there were things happening that were being expressed in play but were very difficult to put together. Then you had interviews with the parents to get a feeling for what was happening, what was going on and things like that. You always respected the confidentiality of the child, but you found the information that may allow you to understand what the play meant at that point, if you were totally lost.

"We did some parental guidance but you were careful with that. You assess the parents' ability to listen without getting too upset or trying to interfere or becoming jealous or destructive. If that were to occur, you'd still do it but with a different person rather than doing it yourself to avoid the possible complications that such things may create. Because some parents really are behaving in atrocious ways, not because they are bad people, but because they have neurotic conflicts that force them in that direction and so they can't listen to advice. So whatever you tell them is going to fall in a leaking basket. In that case, we may recommend that they go into treatment with somebody or some form of psychotherapy. Occasionally we had simultaneous analyses of parents and children. We had some research projects like that, where we had a number of children that were in analysis and we had one or another of the parents in analysis—on some occasions both of them in analysis and that was coordinated. For example, let's say we have one such case with two analysts. The one of the child will come and report to me and the one of the parent will come and report to me. They never talk to each other about the data that they collected from either the child or the parent. I would put it together."

Humberto Nágera in the Hampstead Clinic dining room (1964)

Humberto Nágera with the children in the Hampstead Clinic Nursery

---

DOCUMENT 30   ANNA FREUD

[London]

[Date not included but apparently July 1964]

Mr. Philip Sapir
Chief,
Research Grants and Fellowships Branch

National Institute of Mental Health
Department of Health Education and Welfare
National Bank Building
Bethesda 14 Maryland

Dear Mr. Sapir,

I have pleasure in sending you the Reports on work accomplished during the first year of our grant from the National Institute of Mental Health (MH – 05683 – 02). As envisaged already in our application and outlined in the Summary Progress Report sent in July 1963, contributions to the "Profile Study" come from all departments of our organization, i.e. not only from the specially set up Profile Research Group and Profile-Index Committee but also from the permanent Diagnostic Committee, the Index Committee proper, the Research Group for Borderline Children, the Research Group for Blind Children, the Educational Unit, etc. This multiplicity of contributors explains the bulky appearance of the Report to which, I hope, you will not object.

By the time we received the favorable answer to our application from the NIMH in June 1962, my provisional profile for the "Assessment of Childhood Disturbances" had been accepted for publication by the "Psychoanalytic Study of the Child" (an annual published by International Universities Press, New York) in the form in which it had been included in the application. (Reprint enclosed in the Report, Part I, 1). Also the "Profile" itself has been extended by including some "Lines of Development" as described in my paper "The Concept of the Lines of Development" (see Part II, 1) With the aid of the grant we began immediately to proceed with the intended further work based on both these papers and with investigations devoted to some clinical and theoretical problems implied in it. The results of our efforts are represented in the Report in the following manner:

a) The usefulness of the Diagnostic Profile is reviewed from the psychiatrist's point of view by Dr. H. Nágera in Part I, 2) from the psychiatric social worker's point of view in Part I, 3)

b) The application of the "Lines of Development" is illustrated in three clinical cases in Part II, 2.

A specific clinical problem connected with one of these lines is treated independently in a paper by Dr. L. Frankel in Part II, 3).

c) The practical usefulness of the Diagnostic Profile was tested by applying it to 24 new cases accepted in the clinic for diagnostic examination. Of these, 3 cases were selected as samples and are included in Part III a).

d) The method of assessment by means of the Profile was extended from typical cases to atypical ones, using children blind from birth and borderline-psychotic children as examples. This was carried out on 4 cases of which 2 are included as samples in Part III b and Part IV 1).

e) The correctness or incorrectness of our diagnostic assessments by the Profile was investigated by re-discussion of the Profiles after an initial term of treatment. Such reassessments were carried out in 15 cases of which 3 samples are included in Part IV (II), Part V, 1) and 2).

f) A possible use of the Profile as a tool leading beyond diagnostic considerations to clinical and theoretical findings is illustrated in Part IV, especially I (IV/III)

g) The mutual benefit derived from cooperation between profile study and indexing of analytic material is illustrated in the detailed study of one particular case, carried out by Dr. J. Bolland and given in Part VI 1, 2, 3, 4.

h) Finally, but certainly not least in importance, are the theoretical problems encountered whenever the various parts of a child's personality structure are assessed. An example of this is "The Ego Ideal and the Ideal Self" by Dr. J. Sandler, A. Holder and Meers and included in Part I, 4).

Plans for future theoretical and clinical papers are outlined by Dr. J. Sandler and Dr. L. Frankel and I. Hellman in Part VII, a) and b).

I should be very glad to know from you whether this form of Progress Report meets with your requirements or whether you would like us to make any substantial changes in next year's report.

With my best regards,
yours sincerely [1]

1. Anna Freud wrote this but this draft is unsigned

DOCUMENT 31   JOSEPH J. MICHAELS

Joseph J. Michaels, M.D. [1]
115 Beatrice Circle
Belmont, Massachusetts

July 20, 1964

Dear Dr. Nágera,

I was delighted to receive the draft of "Diagnostic Profile for the Assessment of the Adult Personality" prepared by Miss Freud, Mr. Freud and yourself. The Profile is an excellent presentation and what I have to offer are certain minor suggestions which may help to elaborate and round it out further.

In order to obtain the material on which to base such a profile it would probably require a number of diagnostic interviews. If the Profile were to be used later for statistical purposes, it may be worthwhile to list a few significant items which should always be checked as present or absent for later comparative studies. There might be a place to indicate simple clear-cut census data, such as sex, age, marital status (children), ethnic group, religion, occupation, and level of education.

Now for specific considerations [2]:

I. I would include problems of acting out.

II. Following personal appearance, some crude method of assessing the Body build (asthenic, sthenic, and pyknic) might be considered.

III. Is there any specific history of mental illness of a hereditary nature, for example, manic-depressive psychosis? In regard to the personal history some statement as to how developmental crises have been weathered, for example, adolescence and pregnancy. Previous therapeutic efforts? Specific mention as to medical, surgical operations, hospitalization. History of prolonged thumb-sucking, enuresis, speech defects and nightmares, temper tantrums. These are, I think, significant indices of neurotic behavior.

V. (b) i. To what extent has there been a separation of the self, symbiotic, individuation-separation, distinction of inside and outside, problems of identity.

(b) ii. Problems of compulsive masturbation.

2) Aggression, Degree of Fusion of Instincts or Defusion

V.B. (a) Capacity for reality testing. Symptoms, ego-syntonic or ego-dystonic.

(b) Specify type of language (concrete or abstract)

Following B, some considerations of the self, body image, attitude towards illness, attitude towards self.

C. Would include some assessment of style of personality, native intelligence, special talents, creativity.

VI. Would include psychosomatic conditions after "neuroses."

VII. (a) Assessment of action tendencies and acting out.

VIII. I have the impression that the assessment of the chances of the individual to profit by psychoanalysis is based on the paradigm of a neurosis. I think this should be made explicit or further elaborated as to patients who fall within "the widening scope of analysis." In the latter instance, patients who are border-line and who have ego defects could benefit if their reality orientation were improved or if there were encapsulation of any psychotic core.

(a) Degree of ego intactness.

I have spoken to a colleague of mine, Dr. Charles Malone, about trying to apply the present profile to a patient whom he had in control with me. In the process we might be able to test the breadth of the profile and we will be glad to let you know.

With best wishes to you all. We shall be interested to learn of further developments on this exciting venture.

Sincerely yours,
Joseph J. Michaels M.D.

P.S. Would you kindly send me another copy of the draft thanks JJM

1. Joseph J. Michaels, MD was a psychoanalyst at the Boston Psychoanalytic Society and Institute. When Dr. Nágera gave his presentation on Obsessional

Neurosis at the International Psychoanalytical Association Congress in Amsterdam in 1965, Joseph J. Michaels was one of the discussants.
2. The Roman numerals, letters and numbers refer to items in the Adult Profile.

—⚹—

DOCUMENT 32   RICHARD F. STERBA

Richard F. Sterba M.D. [1]
861 Whittier Boulevard
Grosse Pointe, Michigan

July 23, 1964

Dear Dr. Nágera,

I have to apologize for writing you so late in response to your kindness of sending me samples of the work of your team. I am very much impressed by it. I know from my former work on the dictionary what a tremendous task you all have undertaken. I received yesterday Vol. XXII of the Standard Edition wherein Freud's preface [2] to my dictionary is printed and I thought how much more you deserve the praise which Freud was kind enough to bestow on my modest attempt! What I find particularly valuable in your articles is the careful genetic presentation of the concepts which elucidates the historical developmental changes of the significance of the terms.

I hope you don't mind if I suggest the correction of one sentence. On page 18 of your article on autoerotism, where you say: "The lack of awareness and organization typical of the previous phase (auto-erotism) is now modified." Some readers may object to the "modification of a lack" although I understand what you mean. This is a minor blemish, but one would like to see a work accomplished with so much labor and care as perfect as possible.

I thank you once more for letting me read the articles.

With cordial greetings,
Sincerely,
Richard Sterba, M.D.

1. Richard Sterba, MD (1898–1989) was a Viennese psychoanalyst who had direct contact with Sigmund Freud and attended his seminars. In January 1937 a German psychoanalyst, Felix Boehm, gave a report on the nature of psychoanalytic training in Nazi Germany to some members of the Vienna Psychoanalytic Society including Sigmund Freud and Anna Freud. Richard Sterba was there, as well, and recalled that Boehm tried to convey the openness of psychoanalytic training by saying he would be happy to invite a member of the Vienna Psychoanalytic Society to lecture in Berlin. Freud, knowing Boehm couldn't invite a Jewish analyst, asked, "Whom would you invite?" Boehm answered, "Dr. Sterba, for example." Freud looked at Sterba, who replied graciously, "I will gladly accept an invitation after one of my Jewish Viennese colleagues has been invited to speak at the Berlin Institute." That, of course, was the end of that (Sterba, 1982, p. 156). Sterba tied his fate to that of his Jewish colleagues, immigrated to the United States, and practiced for many years in Detroit, Michigan, where Dr. Nágera recalled meeting him personally many years later.
2. Freud's preface to Richard Sterba's *Dictionary of Psychoanalysis* is actually a short letter, and the first part of that letter contains the praise that Sterba felt Nágera deserved more than he:
"July 3, 1932
Dear Dr. Sterba,
Your Dictionary gives me the impression of being a valuable aid to learners and of being a fine achievement on its own account. The precision and correctness of the individual entries is in fact of commendable excellence." (Freud, 1932, S.E. XXII, p. 253)

DOCUMENT 33   ANNA FREUD

Far End
Walberswick

August 1, 1964

Dear Dr. Nágera,

I found Dr. Michaels' letter interesting and most of his points worth considering. I shall take them in detail:

I. 'Problems of acting out' might be added after clashes with the environment.

II. Body build might be added after 'personal appearance' but is really covered by it.

III. Why not add 'heredity' after 'family (past and present)? It really belongs to the family history.

V. b) I: Seems too detailed to me.

b) II: Yes, 'masturbation' should be included but where? Surely not under 'cathexis of objects'.

2) We might make a point d) 'according to its state of fusion or defusion with libido'. What do you think?

V. B. a) This must be a misunderstanding, does not belong.

b) Can be characterized but not really necessary.

Following B etc.: No, this is included already.

C. This should be under II already.

VII a) This does not belong here in the strict sense and would blur the picture.

VIII. There is sense in this, esp.[ecially] in the mention of 'intactness of the ego' (compare Eissler) and the nearness to or distance from the neurotic pattern.

With best regards,
Yours sincerely
Annafreud

DOCUMENT 34   DOROTHY BURLINGHAM

Far End
Walberswick

August 13, 1964

Dear Dr. Nágera,

I have just received a copy of the letter [one of the Hampstead Clinic analysts] sent you in criticism of your paper on the Blind. I was astounded at the fierce tone. I hope that you have not taken it as amiss as I have. Perhaps it is good to know the strength of emotions, and be aware before too much is involved and keep the scientific work going on peacefully and steadily. I am sure that is your intention. I am fascinated by the possibilities that this study on the blind, gives us, especially the inconsistencies of the material.

I do hope that these summer weeks in London have been some kind of a holiday for you and your family.

Yours sincerely
Dorothy Burlingham

DOCUMENT 35   ANNA FREUD

Far End
Walberswick

August 16, 1964

Dear Dr. Nágera,

I thought you might be interested in the following: I am in correspondence with the Indian analyst Dr. K. Bose (nephew of the original R. Bose [1] who wrote a big book about the Theory of Conflict). I have just written him a long letter and in it also promised that you would send him your paper on 'Fixation and Regression' [2], and perhaps tell him about other work which we are doing in this direction. He might be interested in your paper on the Blind. He seems to have a very open mind in some directions and be rather confused in others, but, I think, worth taking some trouble about.

I enclose also a Note by Strachey which will introduce the papers on Hypnotism in the Collected Papers and which you may find useful in your historical studies.

In your letter of August 6th you asked whether I have sent the Adult Profile to the US. I have not done so since Ruth Eissler and all the other editors are on holiday now and absent. But, anyway, since there is no hurry with publication, don't we want to insert all the additions first?

This is very much a working holiday, I find!

Yours sincerely
Annafreud

1. Anna Freud refers to K. Bose as an Indian analyst and says his uncle was the "the original R. Bose." But she got the uncle's first initial wrong, as it was Girindrasekhar Bose (1886–1953), who wrote *Concept of Repression* (1921), served as the first president of the Indian Psychoanalytic Society, and maintained a correspondence with Sigmund Freud from 1921–1937.
2. "Fixation and Regression" was published in Nágera's *The Developmental Approach to Child Psychopathology* (1981), New York: Jason Aronson, pp. 51–69.

DOCUMENT 36   W. ERNEST FREUD

[postcard]
Highcliff-on-sea [1]

August 26, 1964

Dear Nágeras!

We are having a very nice holiday in Hampshire with a lot of sunshine again. It is very quiet where we are (nice bungalow and large garden). Irene [2] is very busy, I am very lazy, Colin [3] is reading a lot. Best wishes from all of us, to all of you!

Ernest [4]

1. "Highcliff-on-sea" is a vacation spot in southwest England.
2. Irene Freud (1920–2005) was Anna Freud's niece-in-law. She was married to W. Ernest Freud, the son of Anna Freud's deceased sister Sophie Freud-Halberstadt. Irene was a Hampstead Clinic-trained child-analyst.
3. Colin Peter Freud (1956–1987) was the son of Irene and W. Ernest Freud. He was much loved by Anna Freud and played on occasion with the Nágeras' children.
4. "Ernest" is W. Ernest Freud (1914–2008), Freud's oldest grandson and the only Freud grandchild to become a psychoanalyst. He was born Ernst Wolfgang Halberstadt, the son of Max Halberstadt, a Hamburg portrait photographer, and Sophie Freud, Freud's second daughter. When Ernst was 18 months old, Sigmund Freud observed him playing with a wooden spool on the end of a string. He described and famously interpreted Ernst's little game (fort–da) in *Beyond the Pleasure Principle* (1920). Ernst's mother died when he was a boy and Anna Freud became a kind of foster-mother to him. After the war and after his father's death, Ernst changed his name to W. Ernest Freud, partially because he'd always felt closer to the Freud side of his family. He did his psychoanalytic training at the Institute of the British Psycho-Analytical Society, looked to his aunt, Anna Freud, as a mentor, affiliated himself

closely with the Hampstead Clinic, and became a close personal friend and colleague of Humberto Nágera.

—⚋—

DOCUMENT 37   ANNA FREUD

Far End
Walberswick

August 31, 1964

Dear Dr. Nágera,

Thank you very much for your letters. I am so glad that the ordeal of the Psychotherapy Congress is over. You have not missed much, it was all rather depressing in the level of performance. I would have liked you to be there, though, to tell me whether I did all right. I was a bit uncertain about it this time.

I have heard about No. 8. [1] But the price is above £20,000 (!) not counting necessary repairs and that is far beyond even American possibilities. Therefore, I'm not looking in that direction.

Dr. Jeanne Brand of the N.I.M.H. has written that she will be in London at the end of September until October 3rd and would like to discuss certain points concerning our application. I have cabled her that I shall be back on September 28 and offered her Tuesday 29th 11 – 1, to meet the whole Profile Group. I hope that will be all right for her.

I have written to Ruth Eissler, sent the Adult Profile, and asked her to tell us whether the Child Study [2] wants it at all (because of "adult"). If she says no, we shall try one of the other Journals.

My address from September 4th – 25th is "Sadakoti", Glandore, County Cork, Ireland.

I am very deep in writing and enjoy it very much.

Yours sincerely
Annafreud

1. Nágera recalled: "No. 8 was a building that came up for sale in the same street [Maresfield Gardens] as the other buildings of the Clinic, but it was not bought."
2. The annual, *Psychoanalytic Study of the Child*, focuses on clinical work and theory about children and it published many articles by the people at the Hampstead Clinic. When they wrote "Metapsychological Assessment of the Adult Personality: The Adult Profile," in one way it made sense to publish it with the other articles, but its focus on adults didn't quite fit with the focus of the annual. As it turned out, the *Psychoanalytic Study of the Child* did publish it.

DOCUMENT 38   ANNA FREUD and DOROTHY BURLINGHAM

September 10, 1964

Dear Dr. Nágera,

This is a good place [1] for a holiday as well as to work. It's unbelievably quiet warm and beautiful. [Continues in Anna Freud's handwriting] It is always surprising how many beautiful places there are in the world. We are very happy here.

Yours sincerely
Annafreud
Dorothy Burlingham

1. This postcard from a holiday spot in County Cork, Ireland starts in the handwriting of Dorothy Burlingham.

DOCUMENT 39   ANNA FREUD

Glandore
County Cork

September 16, 1964

Dear Dr. Nágera,

Dr. Pollock's [1] letter [2] is very nice. Yes, of course, I am all for his having the Adult Profile and also the Washington Report. It can only be good for us if other people are interested.

September passes very fast, much too fast for me. The writing goes well but I wish I could stay here until the book [3] is finished. It is all planned but it needs time.

The country is simply beautiful and we are very happy here.

Why is the clinic quiet? Should it be? [4]

Very sincerely yours
Annafreud

1. George Pollock, M.D. was one of the distinguished analysts in the international psychoanalytic community offering feedback on the work at the Hampstead Clinic.
2. We don't have Dr. Pollock's 1964 letter.
3. The book that Anna Freud was working on was *Normality and Pathology in Childhood: Assessments of Development. The Writings of Anna Freud,* Vol. VI, New York: International Universities Press.
4. Nágera recalled: "The Clinic was always quieter in the summer with school holidays, parents away on vacation, etc."

DOCUMENT 40   ANNA FREUD

20 Maresfield Gardens
London

November 9, 1964

Dear Dr. Nágera,

You may be interested to see the enclosed [1].
   In Cleveland they use our Profile most intelligently. One question came up which I could not answer: Where in the diagnostic scheme do we place the psychosomatic disorders? Where do we?

Yours sincerely
Annafreud

1. The "enclosed" is missing.

DOCUMENT 41   ANNA FREUD

20 Maresfield Gardens
London

November 13, 1964

Dear Dr. Nágera,

I think the enclosed paper will interest you. [1]

Yours sincerely
Annafreud

1. This is the first of many such notes that Anna Freud sent to Dr. Nágera. Collectively they reflect the close back-and-forth association between

the two while working together at the Hampstead Clinic. Longer and more substantive letters were written on vacations and later, after Nágera had left the Clinic.

DOCUMENT 42   ANNA FREUD

20 Maresfield Gardens
London

December 4, 1964

Dear Dr. and Mrs. Nágera,

Thank you so much for the absolutely wonderful flowers [1]. I enjoy them very much.

Yours sincerely
Annafreud

1. This short note, addressed to Dr. and Mrs. Nágera, is in thanks for the flowers they sent to Anna Freud as a birthday gift. She had turned 69 on December 3rd.

DOCUMENT 43   ANNA FREUD

[Christmas 1964]

A small token from my father's collection [1] to sit as a protective goddess on your desk. Christmas 1964
    WITH BEST WISHES FOR CHRISTMAS AND THE NEW YEAR [2]
Annafreud

1. Accompanying this card was a box tied with a green ribbon and a red card saying "Dr. H. Nágera." Inside the box was a small black stand upon which is mounted the head of an ancient Greek goddess, directly from Sigmund Freud's personal collection of antiquities.
2. Printed card

DOCUMENT 44 ANNA FREUD

Far End
Walberswick
Suffolk

December 28, 1964

Dear Dr. Nágera,

I was delighted with the charming 'indoor garden' [1], and very pleased to have your letter. A good New Year for your whole family.

Yours sincerely
Annafreud

1. The 'indoor garden' may have referred to some sort of Christmas gift.

DOCUMENT 45 ANNA FREUD

Far End
Walberswick

January 4, 1965

Dear Dr. Nágera,

As you know, I work all the time for Mr. Strachey, revising his translations for the Standard Edition. At present, he is re-doing the Project [1] and he has written a most interesting Introduction for it. Since I thought it would interest you to read it, I asked him for the loan of a copy which I enclose here. I think we can keep it about a week, or a little more. (It takes a few months, of course, before it is available in print.)

Yours sincerely
Annafreud

P.S. A letter came just now from Ruth Eissler that the arrangements for the Monographs [2] are approved. Also, that your paper on the Infantile Neuroses [3] has been passed for it by 2 of the editors and is now read by the third, who will do so before Jan. 15th.

1. James Strachey wrote an introduction to his translation of Sigmund Freud's 1895 paper, "Project for a Scientific Psychology." The year 1895 marked the birth of psychoanalysis and the birth of Anna Freud as well. S. Freud, "Project for a scientific psychology" (1895). *The Standard Edition of the Complete Psychological Works of Sigmund Freud*, Vol. 1, Hogarth Press, London, 1953, pp. 283–397.
2. In addition to the annual, *The Psychoanalytic Study of the Child* initiated a monograph series.
3. The full title of Nágera's monograph is *Early Childhood Disturbances, the Infantile Neurosis, and the Adulthood Disturbances: Problems of a Developmental Psychoanalytic Psychology,* and it was published as Monograph No. 2 (1966) in the Monograph Series of *The Psychoanalytic Study of the Child.*

FAR END.
WALBERSWICK.
NR. SOUTHWOLD.
SUFFOLK.

4. 1. 65.

Dear Dr. Nagera,

As you know, I work all the time for Mr. Strachey, revising his translations for the Standard Edition. At present, he is re-doing the Project and he has written a most interesting Introduction for it. Since I thought it would interest you to read it, I asked him for the loan of a copy which I enclose here. I think we can keep it about a week, or a little more. (It takes a few months, of course, before it is available in print.)

Yours sincerely

Anna Freud

P. S. A letter came just now from Ruth Eissler that the arrangements for the Monographs are approved. Also, that your paper on the Infantile Neuroses has been passed for it by 2 of the editors and is now read by the third, who will do so before Jan. 15th.

DOCUMENT 46 ANNA FREUD

Far End
Walberswick

January 8, 1965

Dear Dr. Nágera,

Thank you for returning the Strachey Introduction. Translating the Project properly is no easy job, but he does it marvelously, correcting all the former errors in its first edition and translation.

Your table of contents has made me very curious, especially IV and V. I look forward to it very much.

Even this long holiday is too short for all the things I ought to do.

Yours sincerely
Annafreud

DOCUMENT 47 ANNA FREUD

Far End
Walberswick

January 9, 1965

Dear Dr. Nágera,

You remember that you wanted me to write an introduction to the enclosed paper for this year's Report to Washington. I have done it now and I wonder whether you think that it will do. Do let me know [1].

Yours sincerely
Annafreud

1. Anna Freud exuded confidence and certainty in many matters but she also had a very collaborative spirit and came to rely heavily on Nágera for his counsel and feedback.

DOCUMENT 48   ANNA FREUD

Far End
Walberswick

January 14, 1965

Dear Dr. Nágera,

Your MS. [manuscript] [1] came and I look forward to reading it here still in the holiday peace which will soon be over.

Prof. Frijling-Schreuder's [2] dates are all right for me. As regards material, of course, Dr. Bolland's [3] case will be all right as the basic one. But she [4] also needs diagnostic material to turn into profiles herself, so that you can see how far she understands. (I think one will not be enough.)

I would welcome a Planning Comm.[ittee] Meeting on Tuesday 19th at 12 o'clock.

I enclose also a letter from Dr. Wealer [5] as Program Secretary for the Congress which refers to you. You see what a reputation you have in the U.S. already without having been there. (Please return to me next week!)

Yours sincerely
Annafreud

1. This appears to be the manuscript for Nágera's *Early Childhood Disturbances, the Infantile Neurosis, and the Adulthood Disturbances: Problems of a Developmental Psychoanalytic Psychology*.
2. Nágera recalled: "Prof. Frijling-Schreuder was a Dutch psychoanalyst friendly to Anna Freud and to me. We saw her occasionally in Amsterdam."
3. Nágera recalled: "Dr. John Bolland was the medical director of the Clinic after Dr. Frankl's retirement. Dr. Liselotte Frankl had been the previous medical director. Bolland was a Scottish fellow trained as an analyst. A very nice man, kind, honest and straightforward. Anna Freud wanted him to continue working with me after she was gone. I was to take her place as the Director of the Clinic and Bolland would be the Medical Director. My M.D., degree was not valid in London, and in England lay analysts, of which there were many at the Clinic, needed coverage by a licensed M.D. to see patients. He and I use to fly to Holland together many weekends to teach at the University in Leiden. We were good friends. Unfortunately, he got sick and died quickly though he was reasonably young."
4. Referring here to Prof. Frijling-Schreuder.
5. The Congress referred to was the International Psychoanalytical Association's 24th Congress in Amsterdam, Holland, planned for the upcoming summer and at which Nágera would be moderating a panel discussion on obsessional neurosis. The "reputation" Nágera had developed was probably for the quality of the first draft of his monograph, *Obsessional Neuroses: Developmental Psychopathology*, which was distributed before the Congress.

DOCUMENT 49   ANNA FREUD

Far End
Walberswick
NR Southwold
Suffolk

January 17, 1965

Dear Dr. Nágera,

Dr. Crown of the Institute Seminar has sent me the enclosed Profile of his adult patient and I have promised that it can be [illegible] (or put on the Bande) in the clinic for 15 copies, for discussion in the seminar.

But before that, please would you read it critically and see whether you have any suggestions for alterations?

His examinations will be over by the end of the week.

Yours sincerely
Annafreud

DOCUMENT 50   ANNA FREUD

20 Maresfield Gardens
London NW3
Hampstead

February 3, 1965

Dear Dr. Nágera,

I have just found another passage on the obsessional neurosis in my book (while proof-reading) or have I marked it already?

It is in Chapter V under The Developmental Disturbances: in "A Transitory Obsessional Phase".

Yours sincerely
Annafreud

DOCUMENT 51   GEORGE H. POLLOCK

George H Pollock M.D.
The Institute for Psychoanalysis
664 North Michigan Avenue
Chicago, Illinois 60611

February 22, 1965

Dear Humberto,

I am enclosing some of the comments already received on the Adult Profile, as well as material that we have been using here for some time which is different from your research but obviously related.

There will be several more comments forthcoming and we would appreciate your reaction as well as that of Miss Freud to our particular approach.

Sincerely,
George H. Pollock, M.D.

DOCUMENT 52   ANNA FREUD

20 Maresfield Gardens
London

February 25, 1965

Dear Dr. Nágera,

I have read the remarks and the material from their side. Perhaps we can discuss it some time and think up an answer for them. Of course, their aim of assessment is different from ours.

Yours sincerely
Annafreud

DOCUMENT 53   ANNA FREUD

20 Maresfield Gardens
London

May 6, 1965

Dear Dr. Nágera,

Please, read it [1] so that we can discuss it.

Yours sincerely
Annafreud

1. Unknown reference.

DOCUMENT 54   ANNA FREUD

20 Maresfield Gardens
London

May 9, 1965

Dear Dr. Nágera,

Mr. Meers [1] has sent me the enclosed for reading. I find it very interesting and I wonder whether you also approve of it.

Yours sincerely
Annafreud

1. Nágera recalled: "Mr. Meers was a student at the clinic. An American called Dale Meers. Once he graduated he went back to the States."

DOCUMENT 55   ANNA FREUD

20 Maresfield Gardens
London

May 12, 1965

Dear Dr. Nágera,

Enclosed are my latest efforts for the adult profile. I wonder whether you will find them satisfactory.

Yours sincerely
Annafreud

DOCUMENT 56   ANNA FREUD

20 Maresfield Gardens
London

May 13, 1965

Dear Dr. Nágera,

I think this reads very well.

(I have marked 2 small errors, probably by typist so that she should not repeat them: on page 4 "interfered" and on page 5 "fear of").

On page 3 line 2 the word <u>suspect</u> is open to misunderstanding. I think you mean to say: nothing - - - - that gave either negative or positive indication concerning his ability - - - -"

What about the superego section?

Ruth Eissler asked to have it middle of May. It might be good if you wrote a word to her saying that it is underway, so that she does not print the former version.

Yours sincerely
Annafreud

DOCUMENT 57   ANNA FREUD

20 Maresfield Gardens
London

May 27, 1965

Dear Dr. Nágera,

I think this [1] is very interesting even if not quite as informative as Mr. Holder's.

Yours sincerely
Annafreud

1. [1] Unknown reference.

DOCUMENT 58   ANNA FREUD

20 Maresfield Gardens
London

June 24, 1965

Dear Dr. Nágera,

Thank you for your note. It is true that Mr. Laufer's [1] profile of Joey is a short one but I think it is very well done and we should use it as an example.

Yours sincerely,
Annafreud

1. Nágera recalled: "Moses Laufer (1928–2006) was a Canadian psychoanalyst residing in London. He was on the staff at the Clinic for a while. He ran a free treatment organization for adolescents that was financed by a Dutch Charity. He wrote the Profile for adolescents. Adolescence was his specialty."

DOCUMENT 59   ANNA FREUD

Anna Freud on Obsessional Neurosis at the 1965 IPA Congress in Amsterdam

NOTE: In previous letters we saw how Dr. Nágera expressed to Anna Freud his interest in obsessional neurosis. In an effort to further his interest he began studying all that Sigmund Freud and Anna Freud had written about obsessional neurosis and then examined the contributions of other analysts. He put together a monograph that addressed these contributions and various aspects of obsessional neurosis. His then-unpublished monograph, *Obsessional Neuroses: Developmental Psychopathology*, was distributed at the 1965 International Psychoanalytical Association Congress in Amsterdam on the theme of Obsessional Neurosis. A panel of discussants was assembled to address this monograph with Dr. Nágera as moderator. The discussants were Dr. Arthur Valenstein, Dr. Joseph J. Michaels, Dr. Paul Myerson, Dr. Philip Weissman, Dr. Max Schur, Miss Charlotte Balkanyi and Miss Anna Freud.

Dr. Nágera had the foresight to tape record the event, preserving the voices and thinking of these notable analysts on such a fascinating subject. To hear the recording is to be impressed by the strength of Anna Freud's voice and the clarity of her conceptualizations. The discussants addressed many issues including their own research. It is a fascinating recording in many respects and gives the clinician much to think about, including the environmental and innate determinants of obsessive compulsive phenomena, normal and pathological manifestations of obsessional behavior, the strengths of the instincts and constitution of the ego, the excessive measures of control enlisted to manage excessive frustration or excessive stimulation, precocious ego development as a factor in the genesis of premature and rigid control, and so on. I'll not attempt a summary, but one of the discussants thought it useful to quote Anna Freud's eloquent formulation, and it is worth quoting it here, as well. Anna Freud wrote in *Normality and Pathology in Childhood* (1965): "... while accelerated ego development leads to an increase in conflicts to neurotic symptom formation, and to the obsessive character. Accelerated drive development produces lack of control in matters of sex and aggression, insufficient integration of the personality, and impulsive personalities." (A. Freud, 1965, p. 126) The two-hour audio recording of the full panel discussion on obsessional neuroses is available on the Carter-Jenkins Center website and what follows here is a transcription of Anna Freud's discussion.

Dr. Nágera: I call now Miss Freud. Yes, Miss Freud, so you are recorded and we keep it for posterity.

Miss Freud: I really only have a few questions to insert into the present discussion and besides I want to quarrel with two words that have been used in the morning and also here. One of these is the word "concrete" for the thinking of the obsessional in the sense in which Dr. Michaels queried it now. It seemed to me that this word was used not in the right way but to imply what we would call abstract thinking divorced from emotion, because what the compulsive child or adult tries to bring about is a train of thought from which emotion is excluded altogether. It's the absence of affect and not the concreteness and that is why the ideal of such a highly obsessional individual is "the computer", who can think without feeling. And I suppose all of you have had patients who had this computer ideal. I had one and this played a great part and he tried to train his mind to function as a computer and tried in all sorts of ways to really castigate his body and torture his body so as to exclude the body from the mind. This division of mind and body, or rather emotion and thought content seemed to him the highest ideal, which is, of course, a form of isolation but it goes much further than the usual mechanism of isolation.

The other word is the word "control" and the people from the [Hampstead] Clinic know that I always have some quarrel with that word because it's very widely used now but it seems to me on the point where it's begin[ning] to swallow up defense. And since I'm very partial to the concept of defense, I would like to save it from that fate. When we use the word defense, I believe, we are quite clear what we mean. We mean the warding off of id content, impulse or affect, by the ego. When we call this control, we leave it open whether we, in the concept, also include an attitude toward the external world and towards the objects. Control is so often used in the sense that the child tries to control the parents, as you say. But when we use the same term for the attempt to dominate the objects and for the attempt to keep id content from entering into ego, I think we create confusion rather than clarifying matters. And I would like to ask Dr. Myerson, why he prefers the wider and less clear concept of control to that of defense. I am sure there is a reason for it. And the third question I wanted to ask really Dr. Valenstein, is why in the discussion—I read the notes of the discussion too—why in the discussion so far as compulsion manifestations in childhood is concerned, why you excluded the transitory aspect of these phenomena. It seems to me that this is an attitude very easily taken by analysts of adults when they turn to the study of childhood and especially if they do so by the first of the methods you mentioned namely by applying the theoretical concepts as we had them already. It seems to me that where as these phenomena are fairly stable where we meet them in adults, as you say, "Once and obsessional, he will never be an hysteric" That this does not apply in the same way to children where in one phase —and you find that in Dr. Nágera's description very clearly—wherein one phase you get a profusion almost of obsessional styles, as you call it now, of obsessional modes of warding off content and to your surprise you get simultaneously or a little later or a little earlier hysterical ones or others or real somatization. There is a fluidity of these reactions in childhood, which I think we should not neglect and overlook because it's one of the main contrasts between the normal as well as the pathological manifestations in children and in adults.

Dr. Nágera: Thank you very much, Miss Freud.

The panelists discussed further.

Dr. Nágera: Miss Freud.

Miss Freud: I couldn't agree more with what Dr. Valenstein says, so far as adults are concerned, but the surprising phenomenon with children is that through development the impulses or the component instincts which arouse conflicts change and the cognitive mode over the ego defenses change with it, which, of course, would confirm the idea of the tie between certain forms of defense and certain forms of danger. Well, this would not be the case if the individual is already committed to this particular defense in the sense you said before. Some individual children can be very early committed to, well, selected defenses and neglect the others. But others who haven't made the same strict commitment change their mode of defense with the danger. And we see it after all in the change from preadolescents to adolescents once more where there is a similar fluidity with a different instinctual content coming to the fore. What has come before is certainly gone and you ask where is it? And if for some reason the same instinctual danger turns up again, the child would again revert to the same mode of defense. This is certainly what one can see in observation, on the one hand, of course, in the analysis of children but in the longitudinal observation of children, [as well]. And if I can go on, if I can go back once more to your [unclear recording] observation, I think what you have observed there in this child is a particular stage of intellectual of [unclear recording] development which Hartmann has characterized very well and characterized as distinct from the inner drive altogether. It has nothing to do with it. The child has not yet entered toilet training or anything of the kind. But at least that's what Hartmann says, usually in normal development or what we expect to happen and expect in development, these two things coincide. The child doesn't arrive at this type of mastery of his inner thought world before he has arrived also at the inner problems. Well, the inner problems depend very much on the environmental circumstances. And then in certain children especially those when ego development is very good and very forward you get these types of mastery and orderliness long before the anal phase.

Dr. Valenstein interjected.

Miss Freud: This is, I think, something all children go through, at one time or another, only as with all of these developmental trends not all children do the same in the same intensity, some more and some less and your question would really be whether these quantitative differences—which are also chronological differences, a little earlier, a little later—whether they lean a little later to the commitment to one or the other character style, which then remains. And that is the question and that can only be solved really by very extensive observation. You know I have a question of a similar kind, which goes a little beyond the framework of the obsessional neurosis. I call it "general characteristics". Are there characteristics in children from the beginning, which enter later and are used in character formation? I looked for them in the area of, well, frustration tolerance. We know that there is an enormous difference in how children can wait already in the earlier stages, before really control and mastery is established. The same I believe is there in the attitude toward anxiety. How much can they take? And those who can take less are much more in danger neurotically, because they have to use defense in the exaggerated way. And I think the same is even true in the tendency to progress or regress. But we don't know yet, and we are trying very hard to find out, is it there from the beginning or is it produced through the handling in the first year of life? And at what time is it made use of by one or the other complex mechanisms that leads into neurosis. And I think in all these elements there, that Dr. Nágera has described for the obsessional neurosis, this is really the way it begins. They are there normally. They are there as transitional phenomena, accompanying phase development. But there is a little more or a little less, they come earlier, they come later, they come together with different bits of drive development. And then we get the mixture and then we have to analyze the mixture. But it's not as it looks when you look at the ego.

Dr. Max Schur offered his discussion.

Miss Freud: I would like to say two things.

Dr. Nágera: Yes, certainly Miss Freud.

Miss Freud: They both concerned the difference between childhood and adulthood so far as neurosis is concerned. I think it's absolutely true that every adult obsessional patient has been obsessional already in his childhood. And every adult phobia has had phobic episodes in childhood. But this is not reversible [This is not true the other way around.]. There are many more childhood phobias and childhood obsessional phenomena than parallel disturbances in adulthood. And I think much confusion is caused by the reversal of what we know from reconstruction in analysis. We can always reconstruct a past of the same kind but we can't predict it. That's one thing and the other is a very curious phenomena, which fits with what Dr. Schur said just now. When one analyzes an adult obsessional neurosis and a very severe adult obsessional neurosis, the next phase one gets to is the phobic phase. And we know that this is a very good sign. We've gone behind it. But when you have a child with a real infantile obsessional neurosis in analysis—let us say five or six—what you get next in analysis, and very soon, is not a phobia. You get an impulsive character. And if you asked an adult analyst "How long will it take you in analysis to turn your obsessional patient into an impulsive one?" you would say "Years, if ever!" Well, we guarantee in the clinic in a fortnight. You have to be extremely careful when analyzing an infantile obsessional because you get the wildest acting out sadistic and dirty child in no time. And this has always fascinated me because on the other hand, we see, when we study the obsessional neurosis in childhood, the careful build up of the structures. They look like [they're] eternal. They are so well founded. They remind us so of the adult but they can also move. And I think that's what the adult analysts are not prepared for—for these differences, which really means the fluidity. On the one hand, the dependence on the inner change of instinctive development, on the other hand, dependence on the environment.

Dr. Nágera: Well, I want to thank you for your comments.

You must realize this is just the beginning of what we hope will be a long process of research on this subject of obsessional neurosis. When we did this, my colleagues and I at the [Hampstead] Clinic felt that this was a job to be done. We have to start with this review of the literature and so on. And with the organization of some of the material, we have had the opportunity to observe. But we are far from satisfied with it. We are just beginning. We hope that things will follow from here. But you will remember in the program we said that we hope that this will be an exercise in international cooperation because no institution, certainly no individual, can have enough experience of cases. So I feel that if we could keep a channel open for communication between us, we will able to collect a great deal of material and make it available to each other and in this way perhaps we will be able to produce some of the answers that some of us have [to the questions we have] in mind. So I hope that at least some of you will be encouraged to communicate frequently. Certainly I am a good correspondent so you will hear from me anyhow. Thank you, very much [1].

1. Anna Freud's summary of the IPA Congress in Amsterdam on Obsessional Neurosis was hailed as an outstanding contribution and was published in both the *International Journal of Psychoanalysis*, 47:116–122 (1966) as well as in *The Writings of Anna Freud,* Volume V, pp. 242–261 (1969). It is titled "Obsessional Neurosis: A Summary of Psychoanalytic Views."
Dr. Nágera's 1965 IPA monograph was developed to include material from the Amsterdam Congress and later developments. It was published as *Obsessional Neuroses: Developmental Psychopathology* in 1976.

Dr. Humberto Nágera and Dr. John Bolland

Humberto Nágera and Aggie Bene—Colleagues at the Hampstead Clinic" pictured here at the 1965 IPA Congress in Amsterdam

DOCUMENT 60   ANNA FREUD

Far End
Walberswick

August 10, 1965

Dear Dr. Nágera,

I am returning your letters referring to the Concept Group. I am very glad that we got such an excellent committee [1] together.

I returned from the Congress [2] rather tired, but with a good impression. The whole level was much better than on some previous ones [3].

Now I'm trying to get rested. I hope you enjoyed it all.

Yours sincerely
Annafreud

1. This was referring to the committee of international advisers: Hartmann, Sterba, Greenson, Lorand, etc. The Concept Group members at the Hampstead Clinic over these years included: Sheila Baker, Alice Colonna, Eleanor Dansky, Rose Edgcumbe, Elsa First, Audrey Gavshon, Alex Holder, Gladys Jones, Maria Kawenoka, Lottie Kearney, Ehud Koch, Moses Laufer, Cecily Legg, Dale Meers, Humberto Nágera (Chairman), Lily Neurath, Pat Radford, and Katherine Rees.
2. This is in reference to the International Psychoanalytical Association's 24th Congress in Amsterdam, Holland. The Presidency of the IPA was shared between William H. Gillespie and Phyllis Greenacre. The topic of the Congress was Psychoanalytic Treatment of the Obsessional Neurosis.

3. Anna Freud was highly intellectual and she cared very much about clear thinking and theory, but when presentations were weak, Anna Freud always tried to be sensitive to the presenter and to find something good worth highlighting.

Nágera recalled: "Sometimes people came to the Clinic to visit and gave a lecture. Some of them were good. Some of them were awful. And Anna Freud always took it very calmly and was never critical of these people. In fact, I was surprised. I was fuming at some of these meetings, "What is this person talking about?" and afterwards I remember one day I said, "Miss Freud, I am surprised how kind and tolerant you are of some people that deliver this enormous amount of nonsense." And she said to me, "Well, you know, Dr. Nágera, I learned from my father that in every pile of rubbish there is a speck of gold and that's what you look for. You ignore the rubbish. You look for the speck of gold. And that's what you talk about." And that's what she did. She did exactly that. In an awful presentation, instead of being critical, she would look for the speck of gold, and that was what she would comment on. That was typical of her and that was typical of her in relation to everybody. She was that kind of a person.

"I was at The Hampstead Clinic over ten years and I was never, not once, told by her, 'I prefer you don't do that,' or 'Don't do that,' or 'Don't talk to those people or don't discuss with them a case.' No, in fact, I went to Melanie Klein's seminars at the time I was working at the Clinic. Anna Freud knew about that but had absolutely no objection to it. But there were some other people there that did have some objection to this. There was a lady called Liselotte Frankl who was, at the time, the Medical Director of the Clinic because Miss Freud was not a physician, and in England you need a medical person to cover what were called the lay analysts. And when I went to Melanie Klein's seminars, Lisolette Frankl said, "No, I think you shouldn't do that," and of course I didn't pay any attention to her. I knew that was her personal opinion. I knew Miss Freud would not raise any objection to it at all. It was well known that I went to all of these things and I was interested in learning from everybody. And, quite frankly, whether I did or didn't agree with them was not the issue."

Hampstead Clinic staff members Humberto Nágera, Rose Edgcumbe,
Nicky Model and Dale Meers

—◊—

DOCUMENT 61   ANNA FREUD

August 29, 1965

Dear Dr. Nágera,

So far we had enough always with the 100 copies and I think we can spare the extra expense. In emergencies the Xerox can always do copies for us. I am curious to see how the adult profile will be received.

I am very pleased with what you say about the South American colleagues. It is curious about this Congress summary of mine. I did not think it was anything out of the way but I received more praise for it than for many other efforts put together. [1] One never knows!

I have had patients here so far, so the real rest will come in September only. I look forward to it.

I am delighted that you're working on the translation of my book [2] and shall be only too glad to answer questions about it.

Do you know that a number of letters [3] have been found, written by my father when he was between 18 and 20 years, in Spanish to a friend? I shall get a copy of one soon, I have been promised, and show it to you.

Did you have any real summer holiday?

Yours sincerely
Annafreud

1. Anna Freud's summary, "Obsessional Neurosis: A Summary of Psychoanalytic Views" was published in the *International Journal of Psychoanalysis*, 47:116–122 (1966).
2. Anna Freud gave to Humberto Nágera the original handwritten manuscript of *Normality and Pathology in Childhood: Assessment of Development* and asked him to translate it into Spanish. He did and it was published as *Normalidad y patología en la niñez: evaluación del desarrollo*.
3. These are the extraordinary letters of Sigmund Freud to his friend Eduard Silberstein written between 1871 and 1881—that is, between the ages of 15 and 25. The two teenagers decided to create a club, "Academía Española," in which they would write letters to each other in Spanish. The letters were published in 1990, edited by Walter Boehlich, translated by Arnold J. Pomerans. *The Letters of Sigmund Freud to Eduard Silbertein 1871–1881*. Cambridge, MA: Belknap Press of Harvard University Press.

DOCUMENT 62   ANNA FREUD

Rathmore nr, Baltimore
County Cork, Eire.

September 15, 1965

Dear Dr. Nágera,

The enclosed announcement is an interesting addition to the Profiles on Mark Kemar [1].

I am having a wonderful holiday here.

Yours sincerely
Annafreud

1. Pseudonym.

DOCUMENT 63   ANNA FREUD

Rathmore nr. Baltimore
County Cork, Eire.

September 28, 1965

Dear Dr. Nágera,

Thank you for the interesting enclosure about Bob Green. When one can look behind the scenes in this way and know what is behind a producer in the public eye (Green) or a young married man (Mark Kemar), it becomes easier to understand the complications of life.

For the profile meetings I have one suggestion and that concerns the family case [1] Miston

father with Dr. Yorke [2]
mother with James Robertson
son with Miss Putzel
Coordinator Mrs. Ludowyk

It would be very interesting to have a beginning Profile of each member of the family to show what can be seen of connections between their respective pathology now, so as to compare it with later results. The reports available so far are excellent.

I have written four papers here, catching up on lectures of last year and I'm now trying to finish the 5th!

I hope to see you in the Clinic Monday morning.

Yours sincerely
Annafreud

1. The diagnostic personality profile provides a picture of the patient in terms of metapsychology; offers clues to treatment; offers a comparison for subsequent profiles of the same person at different stages in development or through the lifecycle; and finally, could be used as a research tool to try to understand members in a family in simultaneous analyses. In this interesting case, it was a family in which the father, mother and son were all in their own respective psychoanalyses simultaneously.
2. Dr. Clifford Yorke (1922–2007) was a British psychoanalyst who worked closely with Anna Freud at the Hampstead Clinic. In 1978 Anna Freud asked him to take over the directorship of the Clinic. He declined the full directorship but accepted a position as co-director along with Hansi Kennedy.

DOCUMENT 64   ANNA FREUD

Early Childhood Disturbances, the Infantile Neurosis, and the Adulthood Disturbances: Problems of the Developmental Psychoanalytic Psychology (1965) by Humberto Nágera. Foreword by Miss Anna Freud.

FOREWORD

Dr. H. Nágera's monograph bears witness to the child analyst's dissatisfaction with the present mode of diagnostic thinking. As stated by him, we are not content any longer to subsume all childhood disorders under the all-embracing title of an "infantile neurosis," as analysts tended to do in former eras of psychoanalysis. Nor do we consider it an adequate solution to search for our answer to all diagnostic questions in any one period of childhood, whether late, in the oedipal phase, as the classical view sets out, or early in the first year of life, as more recent views assert. Nor are we ready to accept the exclusive indictment of either faulty object relationships or faulty ego development, which many modern authors treat as the only potential sources of trouble.

What the author of this monograph does to remedy the position is a careful apportioning of pathogenic impact to external and internal interferences at any time of the child's life; the location of the internal influences in any part of the psychic structure or in the interaction between any of the inner agencies; and the building up, step-by-step, of an orderly sequence of childhood disorders, of which the infantile neurosis is not the base, but the final, complex apex.

What satisfies the student of analysis in an exposition of this nature is the fact that on the one hand it is rooted in the notion of a hypothetical norm of childhood development, while on the other hand it establishes a hierarchy of disturbances which is valid for the period of immaturity and meaningful as a forerunner of adult psychopathology.

Anna Freud
London, September 1965

DOCUMENT 65   ANNA FREUD

[NOTE: Anna Freud's feedback notes on Nágera's paper, "Fixation and Regression."]

[Undated]

On Fixation and Regression [1]

Just a few remarks:

1) Might not the full title be: "Arrest of Development, Fixation and Regression"?
2) Fixation versus Regression
p. 3 I think it would be better not to use the term "destrudo" [2] which we have never really accepted.
p. 6 This is really the only place where you emphasize specifically that what you have in mind is the distinction between Fixation and Regression in diagnosis, not in analysis. I wonder whether this should not be stressed more, and already in the Introduction.
3) Vicissitudes:
p. 2 footnote "fluid" is misspelt
p. 2 This is a little misleading since you first talk of latency, then of super-ego precursors (which belong much earlier) than of 4 or 5 years of age. Also the fear of loss of love of parental figures would belong earlier.
p. 3 Isn't fellatio always a sign of oral fixations? [3]
p. 4 This may need some reference to Kleinian Theory where this point is made quite correctly. (what and where?) [4].
Another possible reference is to a paper by Paula Heymann [5]. By the picture you describe so well, she is led wrongly to obscure the picture of consecutive phases altogether and to treat them as simultaneous.
4) Would it be possible to have 2 or 3 more clinical examples.

5) The page numbering is misleading, starting anew with each chapter.
6) Very interesting altogether!
A.F.

1. These are Anna Freud's comments on Humberto Nágera's article "Fixation and Regression," which was later published in *The Developmental Approach to Child Psychopathology* (1981). New York: Jason Aronson, pp. 51–69.
2. At one time there were some psychoanalysts who spoke on the one hand of the life instinct, eros, and libido, and on the other, the death instinct, thanatos and destrudo. While libido was retained, "destrudo" never caught on as a psychoanalytic term.
3. In his final version of this article Nágera wrote: "Though fellatio, for example, is a highly overdetermined sexual practice, the importance of the role it plays in the sexual life of some patients is probably closely connected with significant oral fixations and perhaps especially with the sucking component instinct of the oral stage." (Nágera, 1981, p. 62)
4. It appears that this reference to Melanie Klein alludes to Humberto Nágera's discussion of fixation and regression in child development. The view of child development he subscribed to was that proposed by Sigmund Freud and Anna Freud. It is a view that contrasts significantly from Melanie Klein's view of libido development. While the Freudian view of the oral, anal, and phallic stages stretches out across the first few years of childhood, in the Kleinian view the phallic stage and superego development appear already in early infancy.
5. This is probably a misspelling and a reference to Paula Heimann—a distinguished Kleinian analyst. Heimann supported the notion that the introduction of the mother—not as a split object but as a whole person—into the child's field of experience brings with it guilt, grief, and reparation wishes; that is, it brings with it some of the elements of the depressive position (King & Steiner, 1991, p. 525). She said that according to Klein, both the Oedipus complex and the formation of

the superego come about as a function of the internalization of the parents. "According to this view, the first roots of the superego are to be found in the introjected 'good' and 'bad' breast, to which are added the 'good' and 'bad' parents and the 'good' and 'bad' penis; the building up of the superego proceeds in stages concurrently with the development of the integrating function of the ego, until it takes the shape under which Freud discovered it" (p. 526).

DOCUMENT 66   ANNA FREUD

20 Maresfield Gardens
London NW3
Hampstead

November 9, 1965

Dear Dr. Nágera,

I received the enclosed letter [1] from the publishers. Would you have any interest in the book mentioned?

Yours sincerely
Annafreud

1. Unknown.

DOCUMENT 67   ANNA FREUD

20 Maresfield Gardens
London

November 26, 1965

Dear Dr. Nágera,

Since we have to prepare our Annual Reports in January, may we ask you to give us the usual Annual Reports (apart from the N.I.M.H.) for the Clinical Concept Group and the Theoretical Concept Group. I think it would be best to have one main report on the general activities of each group (including numbers of participants, numbers of meetings, etc.) and apart from that I leave it to you which sections of the work (concept etc.) you would like to include as samples.

Yours sincerely,
Annafreud

DOCUMENT 68   ANNA FREUD

Rathmore nr. Baltimore
County Cork, Eire

December 1, 1965

Dear Dr. and Mrs. Nágera,

Thank you both once more very much for my lovely birthday present. As you see, I enjoy it very much and it has supplanted all other pens in my affection. It lives in my pocket. [1]

My holiday is very restful and beautiful.

With best regards,
Yours sincerely
Annafreud

1. This playful animation of an inanimate object (her new pen) was not unlike the playfulness of her father who, when hunting for mushrooms

in the woods with his children and grandchildren, would act as if one had to be quiet so as not to scare the mushrooms away, and would throw his hat over them once he'd "caught" one. In late August 1916, Freud wrote to Karl Abraham, "When I am very tired I continue with writing the lectures. Seven of those on the theory of neurosis are already finished. Also the printing of the dream is going ahead. Two Chinese porcelain dogs are on my desk, laughing at me, I think, as I write." (H. Abraham, 1965, p. 239)

Rathmore nr. Baltimore,
County Cork, Eire.
December 1, 1965.

Dear Dr. and Mrs. Nagera,

Thank you both once more very much for my lovely birthday present. As you see, I enjoy it very much and it has supplanted all other pens in my affection. It lives in my pocket.

My holiday is very restful and beautiful.

With best regards,
yours sincerely

Anna Freud

DOCUMENT 69   ANNA FREUD

20 Maresfield Gardens
London

January 9, 1966

Dear Dr. Nágera,

I read this paper [1] with great pleasure in the holidays. I think it is outstandingly good, and I wonder whether you will feel the same.

Yours sincerely
Annafreud

1. Paper referred to here is unknown.

DOCUMENT 70   ANNA FREUD

20 Maresfield Gardens
London

January 10 1966

Dear Dr. Nágera,

Another very interesting paper [1].

Yours sincerely
Annafreud

1. Paper referred to here is unknown.

DOCUMENT 71   ANNA FREUD

20 Maresfield Gardens
London

January 31, 1966

Dear Dr. Nágera,

You will be interested to see this announcement [1]. I have written and asked for a copy. Helen Tartakoff is one of the best people in Boston.

Yours sincerely
Annafreud

1. Announcement of a lecture in Boston titled "The Normal Personality in Our Culture and the Nobel Prize Complex," by Helen H. Tartakoff, M.D.—a Boston based psychiatrist psychoanalyst.

DOCUMENT 72   C.D. GOMPERTZ

C.D. Gompertz [1]
17 Chepstow Crescent, W. 11
Bayswater

April 20, 1966

My dear Nágera,

I read your v[an] Gogh chapter [2] one sunny (believe it or not!) afternoon and now I want to thank you very much indeed for the exquisite pleasure it has given me. I find so seldom scientific writing combined with artistic sensitivity and in such combination. The writing is in my feeling not only more true but at the same time also more alive which in a way means perfect. I hear you have been in the U.S.A. during the holiday and hope it was rewarding for you.

We must meet soon.

Kindest greetings and many thanks,
Yours C.D.G.

1. C.D. Gompertz was a Dutch analyst friendly to the Hampstead Clinic.
2. Humberto Nágera developed a great interest in the life and art of Vincent van Gogh, began writing a biographical piece about him, and apparently sent a chapter to Gompertz for comments. Nágera's biography was later published as *Vincent van Gogh: A Psychological Study*. New York: International Universities Press (1967).

DOCUMENT 73   ANNA FREUD

20 Maresfield Gardens
London

May 4, 1966

Dear Dr. Nágera,

The enclosed is the paper [1] which I mentioned to you today.

Yours sincerely
Annafreud

1. Paper referred to here is unknown.

DOCUMENT 74   ANNA FREUD

20 Maresfield Gardens
London

May 5, 1966

Dear Dr. Nágera,

Enclosed is the paper on the profile by Heinecke about which you heard. I would be very glad to have your opinion whether I was too severe in criticizing it.

Yours sincerely
Annafreud

DOCUMENT 75   ANNA FREUD

20 Maresfield Gardens
London

May 23, 1966

Dear Dr. Nágera,

Enclosed is Dr. Furman's [1] paper on the profile. It is very nice, I think.

Yours sincerely
Annafreud

1. Dr. Robert A. Furman was a psychiatrist and psychoanalyst who wrote a number of articles on children's reactions to death and their mourning processes. Robert Furman's wife, Erna Furman (1926–2002), was born Erna Mary Popper in Vienna and survived the Theresienstadt concentration camp from October 1942– May

1945. After the war she took her training in child-analysis at Anna Freud's Hampstead Child-Therapy Course. She married psychoanalyst Robert Furman, MD and had two children. She wrote many books about children including *A Child's Parent Dies: Studies in Childhood Bereavement* (1974). New Haven and London: Yale University Press. Anna Freud wrote the foreword for it. Erna Furman also wrote *Toddlers and their Mothers: A Study in Early Personality Development* (1992), which was an application of the Developmental Profile work to toddlers.

DOCUMENT 76   ANNA FREUD

20 Maresfield Gardens
London

June 13, 1966

Dear Dr. Nágera,

I found this [1] very interesting reading and no one can doubt that it contains a great deal of work!

As you will see, I have put some suggestions on paper, and I have also re-written the title page, both to be discussed with you.

Yours sincerely
Annafreud

1. [1] Nágera recalled: "This was a long paper on sleep disturbances that I wrote and published about the 'sleep disturbances' of children. It is in my book, *The Developmental Approach to Child Psychopathology* (1981). New York: Jason Aronson. pp. 271–328.

DOCUMENT 77   ANNA FREUD

20 Maresfield Gardens
London

June 15, 1966

Dear Dr. Nágera,

I am very pleased that you reacted to Dr. Freeman's [1] paper exactly as I did. I also wondered immediately whether we could include him in the Project for N.I.M.H. in spite of his dealing with adults. Only I did not mention it because I wanted to wait for your reaction.

We must think out how it could be done.

Yours sincerely
Annafreud

1. Nágera recalled: "Dr. Tom Freeman trained in London, but practiced in Scotland. He wrote a personality profile for borderline or psychotic patients."

DOCUMENT 78   ANNA FREUD

July 24, 1966

Dear Dr. Nágera,

After thinking a long time about the address, I have come to the conclusion that the best for all our sending is to use the following:

Dr. Jeanne L. Brand [1]
    International Research Programs Section Research Grants Branch
    National Institute of Mental Health
    North Bethesda Office Center
    Building 1

Bethesda, Maryland 20014

Dr. Jeanne Brand will then pass it on to Mr. Sapir.

Please, tell also Mrs. Thurtle [2] to use this address for the air-freight.

Yours sincerely
Annafreud

1. Dr. Jeanne L. Brand was a grant reviewer for the National Institute of Mental Health (N.I.M.H.)
2. Mrs. Kate Thurtle was the Secretary at the Hampstead Clinic, involved in the overall administrative functioning of the Clinic.

DOCUMENT 79   ANNA FREUD

Far End
Walberswick
Suffolk

August 26, 1966

Dear Dr. Nágera,

There are some interesting data [1] in the enclosed. I thought you might like to see it.

Your sincerely
Annafreud

1. Unknown reference.

DOCUMENT 80   ANNA FREUD

Rathmore nr. Baltimore
County Cork, Eire

September 14, 1966

Dear Dr. Nágera,

The enclosed has come as a reprint now. You know it already but you may like to have it for one of the Seminar members.

Best regards,
yours sincerely
Annafreud

DOCUMENT 81   ANNA FREUD

Rathmore nr. Baltimore
County Cork, Eire

September 17, 1966

Dear Dr. Nágera,

You may be interested to know that there is additional material now for closing off your series of profiles of Mark Kemar [1]. I hear from Ilse Hellman that she has just seen him act and attended the first anniversary of his wedding.

You must ask her about it.

Yours sincerely
Annafreud

1. Pseudonym.

DOCUMENT 82   ANNA FREUD

Rathmore nr. Baltimore
County Cork, Eire

September 24, 1966

Dear Dr. Nágera,

Thank you for your letter of September 20th. I am sorry that I was not more precise about the date or time before but I did not have all the data myself. Now I can tell you the following:

Dr. Jeanne Brand [1] is in London since yesterday. She lives in the President Hotel, Guilford Street, Russell Square, W.C.I. Tel. Terminous 8844 room 473. She is attending a conference on "Medicine and Culture" at the Wellcome Historical Medical Museum, London between September 27 and 29. Please try to contact her by telephone and, if possible, arrange times with her. I am free for her Monday, October 3, from early morning to 3:30 PM so that for me she can choose any hour she likes (and have lunch at No. 20). But for meeting the team, I cannot suggest the time since I do not know when people are free: 12 o'clock? 2 PM? (There is no Educational Unit meeting that day)

Please, arrange what is best. She wants to discuss the new application with us.

With best regards,
Yours sincerely
Annafreud

1. Dr. Jeanne Brand was apparently in town to meet with Anna Freud and the Clinic staff to discuss a grant application the Hampstead Clinic had submitted to N.I.M.H..

DOCUMENT 83   ANNA FREUD

20 Maresfield Gardens
London

October 9, 1966

Dear Dr. Nágera,

I thought it might interest you to read this paper [1].

Yours sincerely
Annafreud

1. Paper referred to here is unknown.

DOCUMENT 84   ANNA FREUD

20 Maresfield Gardens
London
Hampstead

October 14, 1966

Dear Dr. Nágera,

When I said that I would be free all Tuesdays in November, I forgot to except the first Tuesday of the month, when the B group meets. But, I suppose, you know that anyway. The other Tuesdays are really free.

I shall look into all the closed cases. I suppose termination has to be fairly recently.

Yours sincerely
Annafreud

DOCUMENT 85   ANNA FREUD

20 Maresfield Gardens
London

December 4, 1966

Dear Dr. Nágera,

Thank you so much for the wonderful flowers [1] they are a great pleasure.

Yours sincerely Annafreud

1. The flowers were a birthday gift for Anna Freud's 71st birthday.

DOCUMENT 86   ANNA FREUD

20 Maresfield Gardens
London

December 4, 1966

Dear Dr. Nágera,

Do you think we should ask the author for a copy of this paper? It might be interesting for discussion in the clinic.

Yours sincerely
Annafreud

DOCUMENT 87   ANNA FREUD

20 Maresfield Gardens
London

December 8, 1966

Dear Dr. Nágera,

Thank you very much for taking so much trouble about the Profile material for my trip. I am very pleased because I think that now I have really all that is needed.

The H.B. Profile of the Adolescent is just what I need. Besides I have Joey, Arthur, Donald, Josh and George. Laufer [1] brought Paul but I noticed that it does not contain the Family Background so it would not be understandable by itself.

I hope that all will go well, and I look forward to being back.

Christmas wishes for you and your family,
yours sincerely
Annafreud

1. Moses Laufer

DOCUMENT 88   ANNA FREUD

20 Maresfield Gardens
London

January 15, 1967

Dear Dr. Nágera,

It may interest you to read this letter from Dr. Prados [1]. He is also engaged in a study of Van Gogh [2].

Yours sincerely
Annafreud

1. Unknown.
2. As mentioned previously, Humberto Nágera had a long-standing interest in the life and art of Vincent van Gogh, and during his training in London he began pursuing a serious investigation of the artist's life. Nágera recalled: "I once wanted to write a book on Vincent van Gogh. And I did. I wrote the book. I was flying to Amsterdam every weekend to teach at the Leyden University and at the Psychoanalytic Institute in Amsterdam, and because of that I had the opportunity to be exposed to some relatives of the van Gogh family and the paintings. It was an interest I had had since I was a child. So I was traveling there every weekend by plane. I said, "Gee, I can use this time to put my ideas together." And Anna Freud liked the idea but said, "You will work hard, but biographies with a psychoanalytic approach are usually very difficult to publish. I hope you are lucky, but it is usually difficult to find a publisher." And that was a helpful comment. She was concerned that maybe I would do a lot of work and I might be disappointed if what I wanted was to have it published. Actually I was not disappointed, since I found a good publisher immediately."

DOCUMENT 89   ANNA FREUD

20 Maresfield Gardens
London
Hampstead

January 23, 1967

Dear Dr. Nágera,

Thank you very much for the reports on the Concept Groups. They are exactly what is needed. The same is true for the Adult Case Research Scheme.

Yours sincerely
Annafreud

DOCUMENT 90   ANNA FREUD

20 Maresfield Gardens
London

February 1, 1967

Dear Dr. Nágera,

What do you think of this case as a "comparison of infantile and adult disturbance in the same person"?

Yours sincerely
Annafreud

DOCUMENT 91   ANNA FREUD

20 Maresfield Gardens
London

February 8, 1967

Dear Dr. Nágera,

I wonder whether you have seen the paper by Dr. Waelder [1] about "Inhibition, Symptoms and Anxieties". I think it is very interesting from many aspects.

Yours sincerely
Annafreud

1. Robert Waelder, MD (1900–1967) was an Austrian psychoanalyst who studied under Anna Freud and Hermann Nunberg. He wrote extensively on psychoanalytic theory and also on psychoanalysis and politics.

DOCUMENT 92   ANNA FREUD

20 Maresfield Gardens
London

February 11, 1967

Dear Dr. Nágera,

My brother [1] sends his thanks. He was very interested.

Yours sincerely
Annafreud

1. Nágera recalled: "Ernst L. Freud was in charge of Freud's copyrights. I vaguely remember this being related to a new translation of Freud's work in Argentina."

DOCUMENT 93   ANNA FREUD

20 Maresfield Gardens
London

February 17, 1967

Dear Dr. Nágera,

Thank you for your note of 16th February sent to the Administrative Meeting through Mrs. Thurtle. I have now written the relevant letters to Mrs. Teasedale, Mr. Smithie and Dr. Johnson [1] and I enclose copies of these for your information. I hope that the three people concerned have made a firm promise as regards their form of reporting to you so that no difficulties can arise from this in the future.

As regards payment for your co-ordination work, I realize that co-ordination for Miss Shruber under the adult project is already included in your salary now. What has to be added further is the co-ordination regarding the Warren case. According to simultaneous analyses condition, this comes to £150 per year and case, i.e. to £ 300 per year for mother and son.

Please notify Miss Weiss [2] whenever you begin co-ordination.

Yours sincerely
Annafreud, LL.D., Sc.D.

1. These were apparently three analysts [pseudonyms] whose reporting on their Hampstead Clinic cases was lacking.
2. Hampstead Clinic administrator Miss Jula Weiss.

DOCUMENT 94   ANNA FREUD

20 Maresfield Gardens
London

March 2, 1967

Dear Dr. Nágera,

I am sorry that I delayed the decision about Mrs. Gavshon [1]. It is all right now, and we shall employ her for one weekly session.

Please, let me know only when you would like her to begin, still before Easter or perhaps with April 1st? It can be done as you wish.

Yours sincerely
Annafreud

1. Nágera recalled: "Audrey Gavshon was a graduate from the Hampstead Child-Therapy program. I wanted to employ her in some research projects."

DOCUMENT 95   WILLI HOFFER and HEINZ HARTMANN
[postcard from Spain]
April 7, 1967

Greetings for you and your family from Spain!
Willie Hoffer

with kind regards
Yours
Heinz Hartmann
[NOTE: Both messages handwritten on the same postcard from Spain]

1. Nágera recalled: "Willi Hoffer was an excellent analyst—a classical, traditional type of analyst—what in England we would call a Freudian analyst vis a vis a Kleinian analyst or a Middle Group analyst. He was an analyst in the Freudian tradition. He was active when he needed to be, he was quiet when he needed to be, and he was very good at interpreting unconscious material and dealing with the defenses. He was a very kind-hearted helpful person really. He was not an analyst who tended to interrupt the flow of free associations when they were leading somewhere. But he was active when he needed to be in terms of giving interpretations or dealing with defenses or showing that you were using that defense to not talk about other things. So he had a very good balance. He was a very seasoned and very mature man with an enormous amount of experience and a deep understanding of psychoanalysis and people. And he was very friendly. He went for the nature of the conflict and dealt with the defenses and then interpreted the content, whatever the content may have been. He was really a first-class analyst. No two ways about it. There were not too many Willie Hoffers around. There are not too many Willie Hoffers around now either. He was one of these people who had a talent for psychoanalysis. He had the experience and had an

excellent education as an analyst. Obviously he also had the good fortune of knowing the Freuds, including Sigmund Freud. And he obviously profited tremendously from that. I think his analyst had been Herman Nunberg."

DOCUMENT 96   ANNA FREUD

20 Maresfield Gardens
London

April 30, 1967

Dear Dr. Nágera,

Enclosed you will find the letter by Mr. Barron with the description of the delinquent case which I mentioned to you. Please, let us discuss what you think about it.

Yours sincerely
Annafreud

DOCUMENT 97   ANNA FREUD

Dr. Donald Oken
Chief, Clinical Research Branch
National Institute of Mental Health
Barlow Building, 11-D-01
Bethesda, Maryland
U.S.A.

July 1967

Dear Dr. Oken,

As Principal Investigator for the Project "Assessment of Pathology in Childhood, Part II. Problems of Differential Diagnosis" I submit to you our Final Report on the Two Year Period of Grant Nr. MH – 5683 – 0405.

Yours sincerely
Annafreud LL.D. Sc.D.

National Institute of Mental Health
Final Report on
Project MH – 5683 – 0405
(1966 1967).

The Hampstead Child Therapy Course and Clinic

"Assessment of Pathology in Childhood.
Part II. Problems of Differential Diagnosis"

I. Introduction
II. Study Aim: Problems of Differential Diagnosis
III. Study Aim: Comparison of the Infantile with the Adult Neuroses
IV. Study Aim: Improvement of Assessment by Profile
V. Study Aim: Improvement of Indexing Psychoanalytic Material
VI. Other Studies
VII. List of Contents

(I) INTRODUCTION

A N.I.M.H. grant for project MH - 5683 – 0405 "Assessment of Pathology in Childhood; Part II Problems of Differential Diagnosis" was awarded to the Hampstead Child Therapy Course and Clinic for 1965/66 and 1966/67. Annual Reports were sent in July 1966 and July 1967, giving a full account of the state and progress of our investigations and enclosing the books and papers which represent a result of works on the Project during the years in question. It is now left for this Final Report to list and summarize the bulk of these earlier enclosures as well as to allocate the individual contributions to the various Study Aims as outlined in our Application.

Altogether, over the two years, the Project has produced 24 items. 10 of these (two books and eight papers) have reached their final form and have been published; 2 papers have been offered for publication, one of them accepted by now; 12 further papers, some of them intended for Monograph form, are still in the process of being enlarged, amended and revised, and have reached various stages of completion.

II. Study Aim: Problems Of Differential Diagnosis

When naming in our Application the problems of differential diagnosis as our main aim of study, we had our own, new diagnostic scheme in mind, in which developmental considerations take precedence over considerations of symptomatology and overt abnormal behavior. What we have devised for purposes of assessment is a hierarchy of childhood disorders ranging in six stages from more or less complete intactness of growth to more or less complete disruption or arrest of progressive development. It was our contention that the familiar clinical pictures of childhood disorders take on a new aspect when viewed from the side of their impact on development.

In the list of contents, attached to this report, the following items contribute to this theme:

Aa1) "A Study of the Psychoanalytic Case Material of a Two Year Old Child" by Bolland and Sandler, describes (by means of Index cards) the disturbance of a boy on the border of diagnostic category II (Symptoms of Transitory Nature as By-products of Developmental Strain) and category III (Infantile Neurosis).

Aa2) "Early Childhood Disturbances etc." by Nágera provides in its first chapters a very full general description of diagnostic categories I ("Variations of Normality"), II and III (as above).

Ab2) "Notes on Obsessional Manifestations in Children" by Sandler and Joffe deals with category III ("Infantile Neurosis").

Ab6) "Psychic Trauma" by A. Freud deals with diagnostic categories VI ("Destructive Processes of Psychic Nature - - which affect a disruption of mental growth").

Ab7) "Adolescence" by A. Freud uses the adolescent upheaval as the prototype of diagnostic category II ("Symptoms of Transitory Nature as By-products of Developmental Strain")

B2) "Interaction of some Variables etc." by Holder, raises some general points concerning diagnostic category III ("Infantile Neurosis").

B3) "Recovery of Speech in a Case of Childhood Aphasia" by Elkan and Weitzner, presents an unusual case belonging to diagnostic category VI ("Destructive Processes of Organic Nature which Affect a Disruption of Mental Growth").

B12) "The Psychopathology of Rages and Temper Tantrums" by Koch and Sandler deals with these symptomatic manifestations as representative of diagnostic category III ("Infantile Neurosis"). The part dealing with their appearance under category II ("Symptoms of the Transitory Nature - - as By-products of Developmental Strain") still awaits completion.

III STUDY AIM: COMPARISON OF THE INFANTILE WITH THE ADULT NEUROSES.

The similarities and dissimilarities between infantile and adult neurotic symptomatology, as well as the links, transitions and transformations leading from the earlier to the later manifestations are treated in the following books or papers:

Aa2) Early Childhood Disturbances - - - Adult Disturbances by Nágera

Ab1) "Sleep and it's Disturbances Approached Developmentally" by Nágera and collaborators.

B1) "On Phobias: by Nágera and Hurry, a study which is meant to trace phobic development from its earliest to the full-grown adult forms. So far, only the historical chapter is completed.

B4) "A Longitudinal Study etc." by Hellman and Hayman, producing early recorded data as background for adult neurotic development.

IV Study Aim: Improvement Of Assessment By Profile.

In this section the most important advance is the attempt to extend assessment by profile to the first year of life. Obviously far reaching modifications of the original scheme are necessary for this move. The problems which arise in the considerations which become relevant are discussed in:

B5) "The Baby Profile" by W. Ernest Freud.

V Study Aim: Improvement Of Indexing Psychoanalytic Material

Besides the indexing of additional cases, not listed here, the Index Committees have produced informative Manuals explaining, defining, and illustrating their working procedure.

B6) Provides a "General Outline of the Index", covering the whole scheme and its rationale.

B7) Deals specifically with the "Procedures for Indexing."

B8) "General Case Material" defines the environmental factors.

B9) "The Instinctual Drives" and

B10) "Ego Defenses" dissect internal factors for recording.

B11) "Treatment Situation and Technique" although planned merely as a guide for recording technical data, gives an instructive over-all picture of the technique of child analysis as used in the Hampstead Child Therapy Clinic.

VI OTHER STUDIES

The papers named in this section represent theoretical and clinical interests of their authors, directly or indirectly derived from the Project, and benefiting the Project in their turn.

Ab3) "The Concept of Structure and Structuralization" by Nágera

Ab4) "Comments on the Psychoanalytic Psychology of Adaptation" by Joffe and Sandler

Ab5) "Some Theoretical and Clinical Aspects of Transference" by Sandler, etc.

Ab8) "Some Thoughts of the Place of Psychoanalytic Theory in the Training of Psychiatrists" by A. Freud.

B13) "Adaptation and Individuation" by Joffe and Sandler

B14) "Developmental Aspects of Frustration Tolerance" by Frankl

1. This final report on a two-year period of the research on "Assessment of Pathology in Childhood" gives an overview of the research the

Hampstead Clinic was conducting during this very productive period in Anna Freud's life.

Nágera recalled: "When I was at the Hampstead Clinic, I had a lot of responsibility for writing the yearly reports for the National Institute of Mental Health. As you know, though we were in London, we were an institution supported essentially by grants from the National Institute of Mental Health in Washington. For many years Anna Freud had this task [of writing grant reports] on her shoulders though many people contributed to these reports. They were the result of the research activities of different individuals and different groups doing different things, yet she had the task of getting it organized and to get it all done on time. This was on top of all her other obligations. She found, in me, somebody who had some organizational skills. I had become a significant member of the Hampstead Clinic, I could write, I was a good administrator and organizer of things, so I took over from her the responsibility to prepare the research summaries and reports and publications and organize them all, in the form of an enormous report that would go to the National Institute of Mental Health.

"She was extraordinarily grateful to me because of this relief that I provided. She had on top of these reports all her responsibilities, i.e., running the clinic, having a practice, and dealing with the Freud mystique and the consequences of all of this, that she had to struggle with. So she was very grateful and, in a manner of speaking, we got to be very close. Obviously I was useful and reasonably capable to fulfill that task and she came to rely very heavily on me. But I never did it totally independently from her. I always wanted to know her thinking and how she would like to organize it and what her thoughts were about how the report should look in the end. She was in the end responsible for all of it, though I was responsible for some aspects of it. So because of that and because I really liked her and liked to interact with her and found that very refreshing, enlightening, and educational, I frequently would talk to her about how the report was going, updated her, and sent her some of the rough drafts to get her comments and her suggestions things of that kind. That obviously required that we communicate frequently, and particularly during the months when the activities of the report went into a high pitch. And that was a yearly event. I was very concerned that the report represent the Hampstead Clinic and the Hampstead Clinic was, in many ways, Anna Freud. I wanted what she thought—being the kind of genius that she was—to be well represented. That was very important to me."

—⁂—

DOCUMENT 98   ANNA FREUD

Rathmore nr. Baltimore
County Cork, Eire

September 2, 1967

Dear Dr. Nágera,

Thank you very much for the book [1]. I was very pleased to see it in its final form and I hope that it will be a real success.

I arrived here yesterday, very glad to be at peace. When do you leave for the U.S. and when can we expect you back? [2] I am curious to know what your impressions will be.

Yours sincerely Annafreud

1. The book referred to was Nágera's newly published *Vincent van Gogh: A Psychological Study* (1967). New York: International Universities Press, with a foreword by Anna Freud.
2. At this point Anna Freud was almost 72 years old and looking to leave the Clinic in able hands. She had hoped Nágera would take over as Director but Nágera's family obligations took precedence. Nágera recalled: "Anna Freud wanted me to stay in England but understood that under the circumstances, I may have no alternative but to leave, which

pained me a great deal to have to do. But my parents came first as an obligation and she understood that. Anna liked the States in general and was pleased to visit occasionally. She had many good friends in the U.S. that she liked to see."

DOCUMENT 99   ANNA FREUD

Vincent van Gogh A Psychological Study (1967), by Humberto Nágera. New York: International Universities Press. Foreword by Miss Anna Freud.

FOREWORD

The letters by Vincent Van Gogh, on which this book is based, have moved the reading public by the sincerity of feeling, the force of expression, the depth of human suffering and the surprising occasional flashes of insight which are displayed in them. If, due to Van Gogh's inevitably one-sided view of events, they do not also forge the links between childhood and manhood, internal and external experience, passion and its moral counterpart, this is precisely what the present author sets out to do. His result is the striking image of a high-minded individual's struggle against the pressures within himself, an image which would command our attention even if the man whose fate is traced were not one of the admired creative geniuses of the last century.

In fact it is the essential conclusion implied by the author that even the highly prized and universally envied gift of creative activity may fail tragically to provide sufficient outlets or acceptable solutions for the relief of intolerable internal conflicts and overwhelming destructive powers active within the personality.

Anna Freud

DOCUMENT 100   ANNA FREUD

20 Maresfield Gardens
London

November 5, 1967

Dear Dr. Nágera,

You may be interested to see this announcement [1]. Do you believe in this discovery?

Yours sincerely
Annafreud

1. Announcement from the New York Psychoanalytic Society–Lecture on October 31, 1967 "On an early genital phase, with an addendum on Genesis" by Herman Roiphe, M.D. discussants: John B. McDivitt, M.D. and Edith Jacobson, M.D.

DOCUMENT 101   ANNA FREUD

20 Maresfield Gardens
London

November 13, 1967

Dr. George A. Richardson
Michigan Psychoanalytic Institute
505 New Center Building
Detroit, Michigan 48202

Dear Dr. Richardson [1],

Dr. H. Nágera has notified me that your Institute would like to receive a formal letter of recommendation for him from my side. Even though I am extremely sorry at the prospect of losing his services, I am glad to provide this and to help him in his plans.

Dr. Nágera has joined the staff of the Hampstead Child Therapy Course and Clinic in 1960, and in the course of a very few years has become a key person among its members.

In the beginning of his time with us, he did (apart from his private practice with adults psychoanalytic patients) a fair amount of child cases of a very difficult nature. He was extremely successful in this, and on the strength of this work became a supervisor in child analysis for the candidates of our Hampstead Child-Therapy Course.

At the same time, his teaching activities extended far beyond clinical supervision. He joined our panel of lecturers for the Hampstead Course where his seminars on Clinical Concepts and Theoretical Concepts in Psychoanalysis became an important element in our training. These seminars were attended not only by students but equally by members of staff and senior colleagues who were inspired by him to enquire into the history and usage of these concepts, i.e. to follow the course of their development through the writings of Freud as well as of later authors. The result of these studies has been accepted for publication by the Hogarth press, London, and will appear in the near future.

Another, not less important area of his work was concerned with our diagnostic studies. Dr. Nágera was the first to respond to the suggestion brought forward by me in the setting up of a Developmental Profile for Children. He furthered its systematic application to all child cases accepted for assessment in our Diagnostic Service. He helped to amend the original draft of the Profile; he was instrumental in applying it to the study of Blind Children; to the assessment of treatment results; to the comparative study of mothers and their children, treated in simultaneous analysis. He is one of the authors of a similar Profile adapted for the assessment of adult patients. For a number of years he conducted a seminar for staff members in which these problems were discussed on the basis of the relevant clinical evidence.

During the last five years, our Clinic was recipient of a grant from the N.I.M.H. in Washington to further our developmental and assessment studies. Dr. Nágera was secretary to the study group maintained by this grant, in charge of the annual reports to the N.I.M.H. and had the final word about selecting, accepting or refusing the Clinic member's contribution to these reports.

I can only say that I found in Dr. Nágera a very welcome combination of clinical skill, capacity for theoretical abstraction and extensive as well as intensive knowledge of our psychoanalytical literature. This, as we all know, is rare. I feel sure that his immense capacity for work, and pleasure in work, will be in the service of psychoanalysis wherever he finds himself.

Yours sincerely
Annafreud, LL.D., Sc.D.

1. In 1967 Nágera developed plans to move to Michigan and the letter of recommendation above is what Anna Freud wrote to support his application to the Michigan Psychoanalytic Institute. Nágera recently reread this letter and recalled, "Anna Freud was kind. Richardson became a good friend of mine. He had kept the letter that was addressed to him as the chairman of the Institute. He gave it to me shortly after he retired."

DOCUMENT 102   ANNA FREUD

20 Maresfield Gardens
London

December 3, 1967

Dear Dr. Nágera,

Mrs. Burlingham [1] and I both had very nice answers to our letters to him. I thought you might be glad to see them.

Yours sincerely
Annafreud

1. Evidently Mrs. Dorothy Burlingham wrote a letter of recommendation for Nágera as well.

DOCUMENT 103   ANNA FREUD

20 Maresfield Gardens
London

December 9, 1967

Dear Dr. Nágera,

Since the end of the year is very near may I remind you that we need, as usual, your Annual Reports, about the work of the two Concept Groups.

Yours sincerely
Annafreud

DOCUMENT 104   ANNA FREUD

20 Maresfield Gardens
London

December 12, 1967

Dear Dr. Nágera,

This is an addition to my letter concerning our Annual Reports.
    I am sorry that I forgot to mention that we need also a report for the Newland Foundation on the 2 Adult Cases which they support in treatment. (The blind girl with Dr. Yorke and the over-eating one with Ernst [1].)

Yours sincerely
Annafreud

1. W. Ernest Freud (1914–2008)

DOCUMENT 105   ANNA FREUD

>20 Maresfield Gardens
>London
>Hampstead
>
>December 18, 1967

Dear Dr. Nágera,

I thought you might be interested in the enclosed announcement. I wonder whether this "Developmental Psychopathology" has any similarity with yours.

Yours sincerely
Annafreud

DOCUMENT 106   ANNA FREUD

In May 1968 Dr. Nágera left London, England to start his career in the United States. Before leaving, he met with Anna Freud and she gave to him a jade letter opener as a parting gift. It was the same letter opener that her father had given to her when she graduated as an analyst in 1922. In those early days an analyst needed a letter opener close at hand just to read the literature. Scholarly books were often bound with the pages folded over in such a way that one needed to cut them on the side or at the top, for example, just to open and read them.

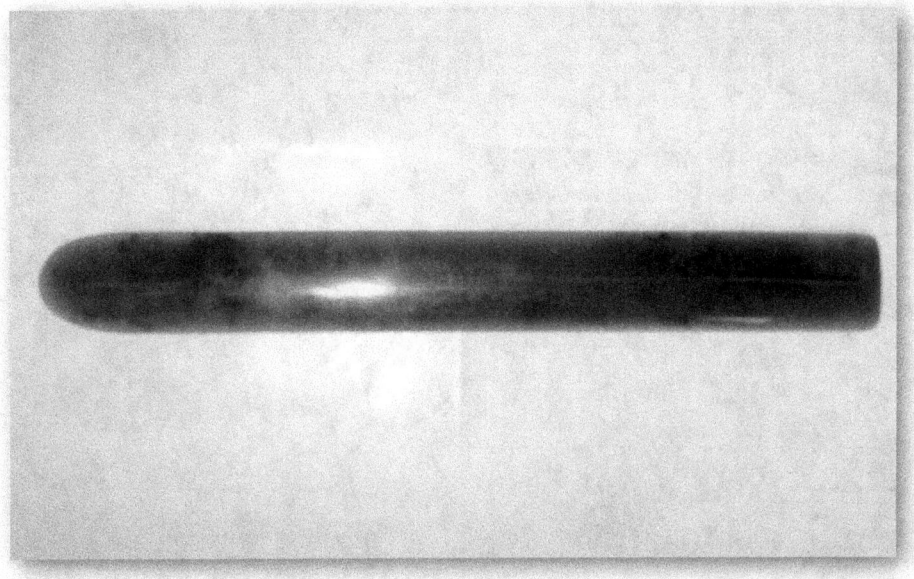

The jade letter opener that Sigmund Freud gave to Anna Freud and that Anna Freud later gave to Humberto Nágera

Anna Freud at her desk in Vienna with her letter opener resting beneath her right hand.

DOCUMENT 107   ANNA FREUD

20 Maresfield Gardens
London

July 20, 1968

Dear Dr. Nágera,

Thank you for your two letters and for sending me the two specimen pages which I return as you requested. Immediately after your second letter, I got in touch with Mr. Peter Leek. He is absent for three weeks now but I had a very nice answer from Mr. Philip Unwin which gave me all the information I needed.

According to Mr. Unwin, they want my Foreword [1] rather longer than expected. As he says "anything up to 2000 words" with a minimum of no less than 750 words. It seems that he will be quite content with the latter and I promise to do it as soon as the holidays begin. I shall send you a copy.

I look forward to the series. Thank you for giving the Clinic all the profit from it. It was all your work, in reality.

July, as usual, is very strenuous with us here. I can hardly wait until we close at the end of next week.

I am very curious how all your plans will develop and I hope for your sake that all will go well. I suppose that the real beginning will be after Labor Day in September. Does London and Hampstead seem very far away for you? [2]

We miss you, of course,

Yours sincerely
Annafreud

1. This refers to the foreword that Anna Freud was to write for the four volume series of *Basic Psychoanalytic Concepts* that the Concept Group had been working on for years under Nágera's chairmanship.
2. In July 1968 Anna Freud was enquiring if London and Hampstead now seemed far away to Humberto Nágera. He had left London only three months before, in May of 1968. In 2013, forty-five years after leaving Hampstead, Nágera noted, "I still miss her and the Clinic—tremendously."

DOCUMENT 108   ANNA FREUD

Far End
Walberswick

August 22, 1968

Dear Dr. Nágera,

I finished the enclosed Foreword [1] last week and sent it to Mr. Unwin with the question whether he liked it in this form or whether he wanted me to make any alterations. Now I have had a very enthusiastic reply about it from him. He's especially glad that in this form it will serve for all volumes of the series, not just for one.

I hope now that you will like it too. I have used some paragraphs from my paper on "Acting Out". I thought this was justified since in that paper I touched on the whole subject of study of concepts.

Now, work will soon begin for you in all earnest. Here we have had a miserable summer with 90% rain, fog and wind. Perhaps September in Ireland will be better for me.

With all good wishes,
yours sincerely Annafreud

1. This is referring to Anna Freud's Foreword to the four-volume Hampstead Clinic series on Basic Psychoanalytic Concepts.

DOCUMENT 109   ANNA FREUD

FOREWORD FOR THE FOUR VOLUME HAMPSTEAD CLINIC LIBRARY SERIES
ON THE BASIC PSYCHOANALYTIC CONCEPTS

Volume I: *Basic Psychoanalytic Concepts on the Libido Theory* (1969) London: George Allen and Unwin Ltd.

Volume II: *Basic Psychoanalytic Concepts on the Theory of Dreams* (1969) New York: Basic Books, Inc.
Volume III: *Basic Psychoanalytic Concepts on the Theory of Instincts* (1970) London: George Allen and Unwin Ltd.
Volume IV: *Basic Psychoanalytic Concepts on Metapsychology, Conflicts, Anxiety and other Subjects* (1970) New York: Basic Books, Inc.

By Humberto Nágera and the Clinical Concept Group
Foreword by Miss Anna Freud

FOREWORD TO THE HAMPSTEAD CLINIC LIBRARY

The series of publications of which the present volume forms a part, will be welcomed by all those readers who are concerned with the history of psychoanalytic concepts and interested to follow the vicissitudes of their fate through the theoretical, clinical and technical writings of psychoanalytic authors. On the one hand, these fates may strike us as being very different from each other. On the other hand, it proves not too difficult to single out some common trends and to explore the reasons for them.

There are some terms and concepts which served an important function for psychoanalysis in its earliest years because of their being simple and all-embracing such as for example the notion of a 'complex'. Even the lay public understood more or less easily that what was meant thereby was any cluster of impulses, emotions, thoughts, etc. which have their roots in the unconscious and, exerting their influence from there, give rise to anxiety, defenses and symptom formation in the conscious mind. Accordingly, the term was used widely as a form of psychological short-hand. 'Father-Complex', 'Mother-Complex', 'Guilt-Complex', 'Inferiority-Complex', etc. became familiar notions. Nevertheless, in due course, added psychoanalytical findings about the child's relationship to his parents, about the early mother-infant tie and its consequences, about the complexities of lacking self-esteem and feelings of insufficiency and inferiority demanded more precise conceptualization. The very omnibus nature of the term could not but lead to its, at least partial, abandonment. All that remained from it were the terms 'Oedipus-Complex' to designate the experiences centered around the triangular relationships of the phallic phase, and 'Castration-Complex' for the anxieties, repressed wishes, etc. concerning the loss or lack of the male sexual organ.

If, in the former instance, a general concept was split up to make room for more specific meanings, in other instances concepts took turns in the opposite direction. After starting out as concrete, well-defined descriptions of circumscribed psychic events, they were applied by many authors to an ever-widening circle of phenomena until their connotation became increasingly vague and imprecise and until finally special efforts had to be made to re-define them, to restrict their sphere of application and to invest them once more with precision and significance. This is what happened, for example, to the concepts of 'Transference' and of 'Trauma'.

The concept and term 'transference' was designed originally to establish the fact that the realistic relationship between analyst and patient is invariably distorted by fantasies and object relations which stem from the patient's past and that these very distortions can be turned into a technical tool to reveal the patient's past pathogenic history. In present days, the meaning of the term has been widened to the extent that it comprises whatever happens between analyst and patient regardless of its derivation and of the reasons for it's happening.

A 'trauma' or 'traumatic happening' meant originally an (external or internal) event of a magnitude with which the individual's ego is unable to deal, i.e. a sudden influx of excitation, massive enough to break through the ego's normal stimulus barrier. To this purely quantitative meaning of the term were added in time all sorts of qualifications (such as cumulative, retrospective, silent, beneficial), until the concept ended up as more or less synonymous with the notion of a pathogenic event in general.

Psychoanalytic concepts may be overtaken also by a further fate, which is perhaps of even greater significance. Most of them owe their origin to a particular era of psychoanalytic theory, or to a particular field of clinical application, or to a particular mode of technique. Since any of the backgrounds in which they are rooted, are open to change, this should lead either to a corresponding change in the concepts or to their abandonment. But, most frequently, this has failed to happen. Many concepts are carried forward through the changing scene of psychoanalytic theory and practice without sufficient thought being given to their necessary alteration or re-definition.

A case in kind is the concept of 'acting out'. It was created at the very outset of technical thinking and teaching, tied to the treatment of neurotic patients, and it characterized originally a specific reaction of these patients to the psychoanalytic technique, namely that certain items of their past, when retrieved from the unconscious, did not return to conscious memory but revealed themselves instead in behavior, were 'acted on', or 'acted out' instead of being remembered. By now, this clear distinction between remembering the recovered past and re-living it has been obscured; the term 'acting out' is used out of this context, notably for patients such as adolescents, delinquents or psychotics whose impulse-ridden behavior is part of their original pathology and not the direct consequence of analytic work done on the ego's defenses against the repressed unconscious.

It was in this state of affairs that Dr. H. Nágera initiated his enquiry into the history of psychoanalytic thinking. Assisted by a team of analytic workers, trained in the Hampstead Child-Therapy Course and Clinic, he set out to trace the course of basic psychoanalytic concepts from their first appearance through their changes in the twenty-three volumes of the Standard Edition of the Complete Psychological Works of Sigmund Freud, i.e. to a point from where they are meant to be taken further to include the writings of the most important authors of the post-Freudian era.

Dr. Nágera's aim in this venture was a fourfold one:

to facilitate for readers of psychoanalytic literature the understanding of psychoanalytic thought and of the terminology in which it is expressed;

to understand and define concepts, not only according to their individual significance, but also according to their relevance for the particular historical phase of psychoanalytic theory within which they have arisen;

to induce psychoanalytic authors to use their terms and concepts more precisely with regard for the theoretical framework to which they owe their origin, and to reduce thereby the many sources of misunderstanding and confusion which govern the psychoanalytic literature at present;

finally, to create for students of psychoanalysis the opportunity to embark on a course of independent reading and study, linked to a scholarly aim and designed to promote their critical and constructive thinking on matters of theory-formation. Anna Freud, London

---

DOCUMENT 110   ANNA FREUD

20 Maresfield Gardens
London

November 4, 1968

Dear Dr. Nágera,

When your letter came two days ago, I looked immediately into my files for the copy of your translation [1]. But all I have is a sample which you gave me, consisting of the first 15 pages. Then, today, I had the idea to ask your former secretary Mrs. Cowan whether she could find a copy perhaps in your former files here, and she really did. I am very glad that you will be spared the trouble to look for it. The copy will be air-mailed tomorrow to the address in Buenos Aires which you wrote to me.

As for Miss Baker [2]: she has never mentioned anything about her plans to me. But, of course, it would be quite wrong for me to stand in her way. A move to the US might mean a great deal in her life and that is a consideration which comes first. She will be missed in the Clinic but it is a gap which has to be filled. Also I should be very glad if you have somebody from Hampstead near you to help with your plans. I think she is very good, especially if she is guided.

Whenever you have spare time, do let me know a little more about your own work. I am very eager to keep in touch with it.

Yours sincerely
Annafreud

1. This was Nágera's translation of *Normality and Pathology in Childhood: Assessments of Development. The Writings of Anna Freud*, Vol. VI, New York: International Universities Press.
2. Miss Sheila Baker was a Hampstead-trained child therapist, and Nágera was recruiting her to come work with him in Michigan.

DOCUMENT 111   ANNA FREUD and DOROTHY BURLINGHAM

[Postcard]
Rathmore nr. Baltimore
County Cork, Eire

December 28, 1968

Dear Dr. Nágera,

Thank you for your Christmas cards and we are glad to know that you are in your own home now. We have come to our Irish retreat for two weeks to get some rest. I hope all is going well with you.

Yours very sincerely
Annafreud

We are so pleased when we hear news of you.
Best wishes for 1969
Dorothy Burlingham

DOCUMENT 112   ANNA FREUD

20 Maresfield Gardens
London

July 24, 1969

Dear Dr. Nágera,

Here is this year's Annual Report for the N.I.M.H. I thought that you would like to see the results of our efforts.

Even though you were not here anymore in body, we felt that you were very much there in spirit and we did our best to follow along on your lines.

With very good wishes for the summer,
yours sincerely
Annafreud

DOCUMENT 113   ANNA FREUD

Far End
Walberswick

August 22, 1969

Dear Dr. Nágera,

Thank you very much for sending me the copies of the contracts for Vol. III and IV [1] of the Concept Group. I am very glad for you to keep the originals.

Have you been in Rome? I do not think so. I skipped the Congress [2] this time and, surprisingly, I was very content to do so. Our summer term was as usually a hard one and I felt quite tired.

We have sent you a complete set of this year's N.I.M.H. Report. I do not know whether it has arrived yet. Do let me know what you think of it.

I still have a month's holiday in Ireland before me and I am very glad.

Yours sincerely
Annafreud

1. The four volumes were:
   Volume I–Basic Psychoanalytic Concepts on the Libido Theory;
   Volume II–Basic Psychoanalytic Concepts on the Theory of Dreams;
   Volume III–Basic Psychoanalytic Concepts on the Theory of Instincts;
   Volume IV–Basic Psychoanalytic Concepts on Metapsychology, Conflicts, Anxiety, and other Subjects.
2. The IPA Congress in 1969 was held in Rome, where Anna Freud had hoped Heinz Kohut would be elected president, but instead Leo Rangell was elected (Rangell, 2004, pp. 147–148).

DOCUMENT 114   ANNA FREUD

20 Maresfield Gardens
London

November 16, 1969

Dear Dr. Nágera,

Thank you for your letter of October 24 with its enclosures.

I only heard about the upset [1] concerning the Concept Volumes after my return from holiday at the beginning of October and then only by rumor. No one told me about it directly, perhaps they would have known that I would not be sympathetic. I must say, I am terribly sorry that this happened after all the work you put here into the Concept Group and its members. I only hope that the justified anger about it, will not cloud your memories of work in Hampstead. Anyway, I am glad you told me; it is always better to know, even if it is upsetting to know.

So far we have not been cut by the N.I.M.H. and the head of our section has not discouraged us from putting in a new application. But will this be successful under the circumstances? No one can foretell, of course. Another happening is that Miss Morrison of the Grant Foundation has retired with the beginning of this month and her place has been taken by Mr. Philip Sapir who used to be our section chief in the N.I.M.H. Miss Morrison was such a good friend to the Clinic and, of course, I shall miss her.

I have just written another paper and I wish that I could discuss it with you: "The Symptomatology of Childhood: An Attempt at Classification" [2]. I try there to group symptoms according to metapsychological principles. So far I have no copies, but they will be made. Would you like to see one?

I have quite recovered over the summer. But I cannot help being 74 by the end of the year.

With my best regards,
yours sincerely
Annafreud

1. Nágera recalled: "A couple of authors in the Concept Group did not want me to publish the Concept volumes with all the people that worked on them named as co-authors, which I had suggested. They preferred that whatever concept they worked on appeared under their name. That strategy made them a contributor to the book, rather than my strategy of making each one a co-author, which I thought would look better on their CVs. I got an inappropriate nasty letter from one of the members of the Group about this, and I found that offensive and irritating. In any case, I always had to review their work and correct it and occasionally re-write their manuscripts. Thus the final form of each concept was frequently written by me anyhow, in most cases

after our international consultants had sent their comments and suggestions. This problem was fueled by the analyst of these two people (they were students at the time) and this analyst was very envious of these publications and my relationship to Anna Freud. It is better to leave him unnamed, though he died years ago. Clearly, the way I had suggested would have been better for them, and in fact I had the right to publish them in any form I wanted, but I liked to involve everyone in every decision I made about the Concepts. I donated the copyrights to the Hampstead Clinic, which then received all the money. The original English editions of the Concept Books were translated through the years, into several languages."

2. The Symptomatology of Childhood: An Attempt at Classification, *Psychoanalytic Study of the Child*, 25:19–41, 1970, and also published in *Problems of Psychoanalytic Training, Diagnosis, and the Technique of Therapy 1966–1970. The Writings of Anna Freud*, Vol. VII. New York: International Universities Press (1971), pp. 157–188.

DOCUMENT 115 ANNA FREUD

20 Maresfield Gardens
London

December 11, 1969

Dear Dr. Nágera,

The clinic has just finished copying my paper [1] and I enclose a copy. I am glad to send it to you now since it will take almost a year before it can be published in the Psychoanalytic Study of the Child. You know how impatient one is as an author to get other people's opinions and I look forward to getting yours. For some reason which is not quite clear to me, this paper means quite a lot to me.

You know how well I understood your reasons for going to America. But that does not alter the fact that I am missing you here and quite especially the exchange of thought with you. Some of your formulations, especially the one about the "developmental interferences" [2] are almost constantly in my mind. Anyway, it should not be too difficult to keep in touch by letter, especially once the first difficult period of adaptation is over.

We have sent our application to the N.I.M.H. but of course the outcome is quite unknown. It is a pity that so much depends on money!

I was very pleased to have your last letter and I look forward to the next Concept Volumes.

I hope you and your family will have a very nice Christmas.

Yours sincerely
Annafreud

1. "The Symptomatology of Childhood: An Attempt at Classification"—see previous letter note [2] for the reference.
2. "Developmental interference" is a term that Nágera coined. Nágera wrote: "A 'developmental interference' can be defined as whatever disturbs the typical unfolding of development. The term may be reserved to describe those situations that involve gross external (environmental) interference with certain needs and rights of the child, or situations in which unjustified demands are made of the child. In making such demands the environment frequently does not take into account the child's lack of ego capacity to comply or cope with them. The disturbance thus introduced may sometimes affect development in positive ways but usually affects it in negative ways." (1966, p. 28)

DOCUMENT 116 ANNA FREUD

20 Maresfield Gardens
London

December 22, 1969

To the membership committee of the British Psycho-Analytical Society.

Dear Sirs,

I have no hesitation in supporting Dr. Humberto Nágera's application for full membership in the British Psycho-Analytical Society. I welcome the fact that he is taking this step, since I am convinced that the work which he is doing will be very much to the credit of any Psycho-Analytical Society to which he belongs.

By now Dr. Nágera is well known in the analytic world through his clinical and theoretical publications in the area of adult analysis and child analysis. He is also well known to the members of the Training Committee of the British Institute of Psycho-Analysis due to his teaching activities. My personal knowledge of Dr. Nágera's activities is derived from eight years of close association with him in the Hampstead Therapy Course and Clinic where he was an invaluable colleague for me helping to develop clinical and theoretical studies and building up an elaborate diagnostic service for children.

I have the highest regard for Dr. Nágera's integrity in scientific as well as in personal matters.

Yours sincerely
Annafreud

DOCUMENT 117   W. ERNEST FREUD

30 Daleham Gardens
London

December 25, 1969

Dear Humberto,

Your letter of December 17th reached me only during the X-mas holidays because someone mixed me up with my uncle, Ernst L. Freud [1] (presumably your secretary). I take it, however, that you want me to recommend you for Membership, which is an excellent idea. I don't think we need bother to check with the Institute about what else is required—the circular you sent to me sets it out sufficiently. The Society needs full Members and I have no doubt that you will have no difficulty at all, especially with such high-powered sponsors as Anna Freud and Ilse Hellman. I am enclosing my letter of recommendation; if you want it altered in any way, please let me know and I will gladly do so.

I was interested in what you write about needing child therapists and child analysts [2]. I would suggest you write out a formal notice to that effect (perhaps several copies) and send them to Mrs. Kate Thurtle with the request to exhibit them on the information boards in the library and canteen; perhaps also a copy to Hansi Kennedy [3], who is during Irmi Elkan's [4] absence dealing with matters of training and advises students, or a copy to Ruth Thomas.

We are held up with the publication of the Baby Profile because (as you may know) difficulties seem to have arisen concerning the viability of the International Universities Press. The editorial committee of the P.S.C. [Psychoanalytic Study of the Child] were in favor of having it as a monograph and I am just writing to Lustman [5] to get the thing moving. While it is under consideration I am somewhat tightfisted with letting copies of the Baby Profile go into circulation. A promise of early publication had led us to believe that in the circumstances this was the best policy.

Generally, we are jogging along, much as before. We are just on the brink of acquiring a little house in Golders Green and conducting negotiations about it has absorbed much of our energies (much as with the first child, you get your experience with the buying of a first house, I am sure any subsequent one should be easier [6]). Private practice is o.k. at the moment, but I will probably be in need of some replacements in a year's time. Mr. Fredricks [7] is making good progress, but at present his wife kicks (too much penis envy and domestic restriction after the [birth of her child]). Irene [8] now works at Kilbourn Child Guidance Clinic, apart from being still at the Baby Clinic [9] with Dr. Stross [10] and running the Toddler Group at the Hampstead Clinic. I hope you and Gloria [11] and the children are all well and are enjoying America. With best wishes to all of you from all of us,

Yours
Ernest

With all good wishes for a Happy New Year!

1. Ernst L. Freud was W. Ernest Freud's uncle, Anna Freud's brother, Sigmund and Martha Freud's second son. He was an architect and the father of Stephen Freud (hardware store owner), Clement Freud (member of British Parliament) and Lucian Freud (artist).
2. Nágera was in search of well-trained child therapists and analysts and looked to the Hampstead Clinic. Nágera recalled: "I had been appointed Director of Child Psychiatry—Chief of the Youth Services at the University of Michigan. That was a program that included 12 child fellows in training in child psychiatry and a Children's Psychiatric Hospital with eight floors, inpatient beds for over 80 children and 40 adolescents, outpatient services, day treatment, schools, etc, etc. This hospital was the first and largest child psychiatric hospital in the country and possibly in the world. It had been built by Dr. Ray Waggoner. He had been the chairman of the Department of Psychiatry for a long time before my arrival there. We were funded generously by the State and could offer services, including inpatient services, to poor people who could not pay for

the services. There were no people with such training (child therapists or child psychoanalysts) in Michigan at that time. The training in child psychiatry was mostly biologically based and I wanted to include a psychoanalytic dynamic dimension as well. After a few years, this program was considered, by most people, the best training program in child psychiatry in this country. I ran all this for over 10 years. Hence I brought several people from Hampstead to the States. That is why you see Miss Freud's comments in some of these letters about some of the people that I had asked her about. Once I stopped being the Director of Child Psychiatry, they knocked the hospital building down to build a cancer research center. The building was close to the Medical School and that was the main reason. They thought of it while I was the Director, but did not dare to do it because I objected to it, and they knew I would raise holy hell by going to the TV, radio, etc. if they tried. But as soon as I resigned as the Director they went ahead and did it. Very sad."
3. Hansi Kennedy (1923–2003) was a child analyst who began in Anna Freud's War Nurseries, worked for many years at the Hampstead Clinic and retired in 1993 from the renamed clinic—The Anna Freud Centre. From 1977–1987 she was co-director of the Hampstead Clinic.
4. Irmi Elkan was a child analyst at the Clinic and Director of Education for a while.
5. Seymour Lustman was a psychoanalyst and protégé of Ernst Kris.
6. The fact that W. Ernest Freud would equate the buying of a first house with the birth of the first child was typical of him. He had a life-long interest in babies and mother-baby bonding, and saw much of life in the metaphors of infancy.
7. Pseudonym.
8. Irene was W. Ernest Freud's wife, who went through the child analysis training program at the Hampstead Clinic.
9. The Well-Baby Clinic was a component of the Hampstead Clinic. It was a place where expectant mothers and new mothers and their babies came for check-ups, exams, and advice in dealing with a wide

range of medical and psychological concerns. When W. Ernest Freud began his work on infant observation it was by sitting-in silently in the mother-infant check-ups and listening and observing carefully the mother-infant bond and communication. His wife Irene also participated in these infant observation meetings.

10. Dr. Stross was the pediatrician in charge at the Hampstead Clinic. When Sigmund Freud left (escaped) Nazi Austria in June of 1938, he was a very ill man and needed to be accompanied by a medical doctor. It was planned that Dr. Max Schur, his trusted doctor for many years, would accompany him, but at the last minute Schur developed an appendicitis and needed an emergency surgery. Freud could not wait until Schur recuperated as there was no telling when the Nazis might change their mind and throw Freud into the concentration camp at Dachau. So, Dr. Josephine Stross, a pediatrician who had worked with Anna Freud in Vienna at the Edith Jackson Nursery, accompanied them to London and spent the rest of her life dedicated to the Hampstead Clinic.

11. Gloria was Humberto Nágera's wife.

DOCUMENT 118   W. ERNEST FREUD

To the Membership Committee of the British Psycho-Analytical Society

December 25, 1969

Dear Sirs,

I understand that Dr. Humberto Nágera is applying for full membership of our society and I wholeheartedly support his application.

Dr. Nágera has been known to me since 1957 [1] as an old friend and a man of impeccable character and scientific integrity. Through our long professional association during many years at the Hampstead Child Therapy Clinic I appreciated his vast clinical experience, the wide range of his psycho-analytic interests and his untiring efforts to clarify and amplify many of the basic theoretical and clinical psycho-analytic concepts. Within the framework of the research program of the Hampstead Child Therapy Clinic I am greatly indebted to his inspiring and stimulating seminars, the results of which have since appeared in numerous publications in the Psychoanalytic Study of the Child and elsewhere.

His combined grasp of general psychiatry and metapsychology proved of inestimable value when Anna Freud, he and I worked out the scheme on the metapsychological assessment of the adult personality (the Adult Profile, 1965), while his contributions to the Clinic's diagnostic conferences on children always reflected profound psycho-analytic understanding of what was involved.

His thoroughness and analytic perceptiveness as a psychoanalyst have been known to me in particular through the seminars of the Freud Centenary Fund Study Group for Adult Analysis (under the leadership of Anna Freud) since 1963, and I was equally impressed by his capacity as psycho-analytic research advisor in connection with my analysis of an adult case of overeating (1966 until his departure for Ann Arbor in 1968).

I would without reservations recommend him for full membership of the British Psycho-Analytical Society.

Yours sincerely,
W. E. Freud

1. Nágera recalled, "Miss Freud gave the date when they employed me [1960], but I moved to England at the beginning of April 1958 and started working at the Clinic shortly thereafter [1959]. I had a student visa and had my own economic means so I did not need a salary. All that changed when Castro came to power and confiscated my money, properties, etc., as they did with everyone in Cuba! Ernest's date [1957] is possibly his mistake. I had been in London in 1957 for my interviews at the London Psychoanalytic Institute but I had not met him. I moved to London in 1958 once they told me they had accepted me for training."

DOCUMENT 119   ANNA FREUD

20 Maresfield Gardens
London

October 16, 1970

Dear Dr. Nágera,

This is just to tell you how very much I like your paper on Adolescence [1]. I was quite delighted with it. It is for my feeling the best that has been written on the subject for very many years, in spite of all the numerous publications which have appeared.

I have one regret only: that it is not any longer a "product of the Hampstead Child Therapy Clinic".

Manna Friedman [2] told us quite a lot about your place and I was very glad to hear it all.

With best regards,
yours sincerely
Annafreud

1. Nágera wrote two papers around the same time on adolescence: "Diagnostic, Prognostic and Developmental Considerations" and "Female Adolescence, Sexual Identity and Homosexuality." They were later published in Nágera's *The Developmental Approach to Child Psychopathology* (1981). New York: Jason Aronson, pp. 231–246 and 247–267.
Nágera recalled: "Saying she liked my paper was quite a compliment. Anna Freud had worked closely with August Aichhorn, Peter Blos and Erik Erikson, all of whom had made enormous contributions to the psychoanalytic understanding of adolescence."
2. Friedmann misspelled with only one 'n'. Manna Friedmann led the Hampstead Clinic nursery school group from 1957–1978.

DOCUMENT 120 ANNA FREUD

20 Maresfield Gardens
London

December 15, 1970

Dear Dr. Nágera,

Thank you and your co-workers very much for your birthday greetings [1]. I had a very nice day and I am trying to feel old now, which is not quite easy.

Thank you very much also for the reprints from the Concept Group which will be very useful. I have received the two new volumes with great pleasure.

I thought you might like to see a picture of my father's statue [2] which has its place now back of the new Hampstead Library. The photos were taken when it was unveiled. The children in the foreground are some of the great-grandchildren of my father. Ernst's Colin [3] was present also but he was busy photographing and did not stand around with the others. I think the statue is quite a success.

I hope that you and your family will have a very nice Christmas.

With good wishes,
yours sincerely
Annafreud

1. Anna Freud's 75th birthday.
2. The statue of a seated Sigmund Freud by Oscar Nemon has subsequently been relocated and can now be found facing Fitzjohn's Avenue at the cross street of Maresfield Gardens in Hampstead, London.
3. Colin Peter Freud (1956–1987) was Irene and W. Ernest Freud's son.

DOCUMENT 121   ANNA FREUD

Rathmore nr. Baltimore
County Cork, Eire

April 25, 1971

Dear Dr. Nágera,

Thank you for your letter of April 6th which followed me to Ireland. I am having a wonderful holiday here for the whole month of April, peace, quiet and sunshine. Holidays are increasingly appreciated as one gets older and especially if, like me, one is ten years passed the official retirement age.

I was most impressed by Dr. Starks [1] Profile and read it with great pleasure. I would never have thought, when reading it, that she is not an analyst or an analytic student. I am delighted that our profile is so alive with you.

I am glad that Cecily Legg [2] is joining you. She has excellent qualities but you will have to keep an eye on her. She is not easily guided. She did some very good analyses when she was with us. Of course, I do not know how she has developed in Cleveland and since then.

Beatrice Samuelson [3] is a very different proposition. I have not been in touch with her since she qualified, which is a long time ago. While she was with us, I have never been able to appreciate either her or her work. It may be my fault, but I find it difficult to imagine that you would find her clever and subtle enough.

Will you be coming to the Congress [4]?

Yours sincerely
Annafreud

1. Dr. Starks was a resident of child psychiatry at the University of Michigan.
2. Cecily Legg was a child analyst at the Hampstead Clinic who went to work with Nágera at the University of Michigan.

3. Pseudonym
4. The IPA Congress in 1971 was held in Vienna and was Anna Freud's first return since exile in 1938. It was nice to see old friends but she also used this opportunity to apply to the IPA to have the Hampstead Clinic designated as an official "Study Group." Rangell says this was opposed by the IPA Council, but rather than voting on it, they recommended it be carried over to the next Congress (Rangell, 2004, pp. 157–160).

DOCUMENT 122 ANNA FREUD

Far End
Walberswick

April 1, 1972

Dear Dr. Nágera,

I was very pleased to have your letter and the two enclosed papers.

You remember surely how awful end of term can be in Hampstead when 11 Foundation reports need to be finalized. Well, it was this way again and it left me quite tired. But yesterday was the first day of the Easter holiday, therefore last night I read your papers.

About "Day Care" [1] I am greatly impressed by what you have written. I think I have not liked a paper as much as that for many years. Most of the neurological background was new to me, as it will be to others. But just this explains so much about our later findings and gives them proper weight.

Now a very important question: where will you publish it? It should have the widest possible publicity and really help to prevent the damage that is looming ahead. Or will you offer it to the Study of the Child and see to it afterwards that the responsible authorities take notice of it? Or that the reviews do? I think it could and should have an enormous impact.

About the transitional object [2]: I found this investigation very interesting and I look forward to the next part. As you know, like you I never believed that the infant is re-creating the mother in this way; what he re-creates is an experience. You really have a unique opportunity for such studies in your setting.

I have to return one once more to the "Day Care". When I was last in Yale, I missed an opportunity to speak out against it. The students, girls and boys, were advocating it strongly and I could easily have made a stand against it. But I didn't. I misunderstood and thought it was meant for the benefit of the neglected ghetto children and realized too late that it was meant wholly to set the parents free.

I am sorry about Carol Peacely [3] but not exactly surprised. Since she had begun to work also for the Tavistock Clinic, she behaved similarly with us, did only what she liked and preferred superficial to intensive work. Difficult to understand!

As regards the difficulties with the University, I just hope that they will not get worse. From the beginning, this was the experience of analysts in public settings. It has not changed much. I was lucky that I was never in that position and wise to refuse when Harvard once offered me something similar.

I envy your children the horse-farm! [4]

Will you be in London in July?

Yours sincerely
Annafreud

1. Nágera's "Day-Care Centers" (1981) was written in 1972. It was a time when economic demands were transforming the one-career family into the two-career family; when divorce was on the rise pushing women into the work force, and when women's liberation was offering women the option of having children and working too. All the factors together conspired to create a rosy picture of day-care centers, which then began popping up all across the country. Anna Freud's life work

focused on the vicissitudes of the mother-child bond and she had personally been in charge of child-care institutions for children who had lost their parents to war and war service. While she studied efforts to remediate the loss of parents within institutional care, when no other option was available, the idea of parents electing to leave children in day-care was never seen as a good idea.

In Nágera's article, he addressed the neurological effects of low stimulation environments on infants in institutional care; the negative effects of low levels of interaction; the problems with changing caretakers; the relation between maternal lack and anxiety states; and more. He recognized the legitimate role of day-care centers in extreme circumstances and offered a long list of suggestions to help ameliorate the attendant problems of institutional care. He criticized the attitudes of liberal-minded and conservative-minded politicians politicizing the issue, and advocated a more disciplined assessment of the situation by experts in the field as an approach to promote the equal rights of the next generation. He wrote: "I cannot but seriously question the advisability for establishing day-care centers on the grand scale that the United States is now planning. I fear that the widespread and indiscriminate use of such facilities, for infants in the age range between birth and two and a half years of age, may result in the United States mass-producing large numbers of children with serious emotional problems and psychopathology." (*The Developmental Approach to Child Psychopathology* (1981). New York: Jason Aronson, p. 454.

2. [2] The work on the transitional object that interested Anna Freud was research carried out under the auspices of the Child Psychoanalytic Study Program, Director: Humberto Nágera, M.D., of Children's Psychiatric Hospital, The University of Michigan Medical Center, and was published in several articles:

> Fred Busch, Humberto Nágera, G. Pezzarossi (1973). Primary transitional objects. *Journal of the American Academy of Child Psychiatry*. April 12, 1973, 2:193–214.

Fred Busch and Judith McKnight (1973). Parental attitudes and the development of the primary transitional object. *Child Psychiatry and Human Development*, Vol. 4(1), Fall 1973.

Fred Busch (1974). Dimensions of the first transitional object. *Psychoanalytic Study of the Child*, 29:215–229.

3. Pseudonym
4. In Michigan, Nágera had purchased a horse farm, was raising Arabian horses, and his daughter, Lisette, was a horse rider and trainer.

DOCUMENT 123 ANNA FREUD

20 Maresfield Gardens
London

October 24, 1972

Dr. H. Nágera
Ann Arbor, Michigan

Dear Dr. Nágera,

You will be quite surprised to hear from me after a considerable time, but I have a favor to ask of you.

At the Vienna Congress [1] I began to think about a scheme of establishing a contemporary library in Berggasse 19, our former home, under the auspices of the Sigmund Freud Gesellschaft. My idea was that this could be done without much money if all the members of the International agreed to participate and to donate their writings [2]. I have now drafted a letter to the members in that spirit, and I got Prof. Hacker's agreement to it for the Sigmund Freud Gesellshaft, and Dozent Solms' for the Vienna Psychoanalytic Association. I did it myself in English and German, and have asked for Italian and French versions from colleagues in Rome and Paris. What is still missing is the Spanish one. Would you do it for me please? I enclose the English draft, and I hope it will not be much work for you.

Otherwise my best regards. We were all sorry to miss you at the Anniversary weekend [3]. May I also say that I feel quite envious of your horse farm! [4]

With my best regards,
Yours sincerely,
Annafreud

1. The International Psychoanalytical Association Congress in Vienna.
2. Nágera recalled: "Miss Freud had made peace with what had happened in Vienna and was glad to go back and start the Library at the Freud Museum there. Willie Hoffer also put behind him what happened to him and his family in Germany, and was going to teach in Germany at the Institute. Promoting analysis made them go, though I do not think they had ever forgotten or forgiven."
Miss Freud did not talk much about being Jewish, it was taken for granted. Manna Friedmann worked with Anna for years, was the head of the nursery school at the Clinic, was Jewish, and was convinced that I was Jewish too because my mother's family name was Perez, and Jews had been in Spain and had been persecuted and consequently hid that fact. My name really is Humberto Nágera Perez. I am sure Manna said this to Anna, but Miss Freud never mentioned it to me."
2. Anniversary Weekend in 1972 marked the 20th anniversary of the Hampstead Clinic.
3. Anna Freud was a horseback rider much of her life, so her "envy" of the Nágera's horse farm was rooted in this history.

DOCUMENT 124   ANNA FREUD

20 Maresfield Gardens
London

November 7, 1972

Dr. H. Nágera
Ann Arbor, Michigan

Dear Dr. Nágera,

Thank you for your letter of November 2nd, and for your quick response to my request for the Spanish translation. I was very pleased to receive it and quite delighted with your quick promise to be a contributor to the Berggasse 19 Library. I take it as a good omen for the response to my circular letter.

It is quite true that I promised to come to Philadelphia at the end of April. But of course that makes it quite impossible for me to be also in the States at the beginning of April. In any case, I expect that my stay in America this time will be a very short one and perhaps I was not very wise to undertake the commitment at all. At the moment I just hope that my health will not stand in the way of carrying it out.

Thank you very much also for your invitation [1]. I would love to see your farm and the horses, but I am afraid it will not be this time. Perhaps another time, and hopefully at a period when I shall still be able to ride, preferably an elderly horse [2].

With my best regards as always,
Yours sincerely
Annafreud

1. Nágera invited Anna Freud to come to Michigan, but she was never able to make the visit. Nágera recalled: "I had organized a meeting in Detroit to raise money for the Hampstead Clinic. She could not come

but sent instead Hansi Kennedy, a senior staff member that later became the Director of the Clinic after Miss Freud's death. Miss Freud sent a nice tape recording that she had made for the meeting since she could not come herself. It was played at the meeting and I was shocked to hear how poorly she sounded. She clearly was in very poor shape."

2. Anna Freud says she would prefer an elderly horse and I believe there is a story behind this. In psychoanalysis, the relationship between the ego and the libido is sometimes metaphorized as the relationship between a rider and a horse. Well, in 1972–1973 Joseph Sandler coordinated a remarkable seminar in which a group of clinicians at the Hampstead Clinic discussed with Anna Freud her 1936 classic *The Ego and the Mechanisms of Defense*. The edited transcription of this seminar was published in 1985. In the discussion about "The Source of Anxiety and Danger," Anna Freud said, "And, of course, there is the differentiation that one establishes in analysis between the past and the present. What is considered a sin in infancy is insignificant in adult life, and so on. Also, with advancing age, the wishes themselves become less dangerous. You know the story of the rider and the horse—well, Grete Bibring once said that it's not only the rider who gets older, but also the horse." (J. Sandler & A. Freud, 1985, *The Analysis of Defense: The Ego and the Mechanisms of Defense Revisited.* New York: International Universities Press, p. 265.)

DOCUMENT 125   ANNA FREUD

20 Maresfield Gardens
London

December 9, 1973

Dear Dr. Nágera,

The gap between your October letter and my answer today is so large that you will find it difficult to believe how pleased I was to hear from you. I very much wanted your personal news as well as your working news and I am very glad indeed that at last you succeeded to do for your parents what you meant to do all the time.

I had heard that you had become Chief of the Department and I was pleased about that even though I know all the burdens of being the administrator from my own experience. But I also learned that this is the only way in which one can have independence and carry out one's plans. Personally I would rather be responsible even for the rugs and the furniture than defer to somebody else who has the power to dictate what type of work or what type of case is worth taking on.

But now to the reason for my delay in answering. At the end of October, returning from a weekend in Walberswick, Mrs. Burlingham and I ran into fog (me being the driver) and when we had to cross the main road, we had a rather nasty car crash [1] which landed us in the Emergency Ward of Ipswich Hospital and our nice Volvo car on the scrapheap. We escaped without broken bones or internal injuries but at our age even shocks to the body and cuts and bruises are not easy to take and get over. On the whole, we were extremely lucky. But even if I could return to work after a week and Mrs. Burlingham soon after, quite a bit of painful effects remained and slowed me up.

Otherwise things are going as well as one can expect in England at the moment. Transport of children to the Clinic is still working, so are the heatings. No guarantees what will happen in the winter. Also the financial situation of the Clinic is all right so far, but I cannot help very often to worry about the future. As you know from sharing it, it was hard work to build up the Clinic and the work as it is and naturally I would wish it to survive and continue for a long time. But who knows? [2]

I am still sorry that you're not here any more, although I always had the fullest understanding that you needed to leave and secure your family's needs. I am happy that this has worked out as you planned it.

I was very interested to hear about Ava Bry [3]. I liked her very much as a student and I thought she had more initiative and working drive than many others.

With all my good wishes,
yours sincerely
Annafreud

1. Anna Freud's biographer Elizabeth Young-Bruehl said that Anna Freud "worried that her habitual fast driving had contributed to the accident," but "the police investigator declared that she bore no responsibility for the accident" (Young-Bruehl, 1988, p. 420).
2. When Miss Freud died in 1982, the Hampstead Clinic had been in operation for 30 years. After her death it was renamed the Anna Freud Centre, and it has already been in existence for more than 30 additional years.
3. Ava Bry Penman was a child analyst at the Clinic.

DOCUMENT 126   ANNA FREUD

20 Maresfield Gardens
London

February 25, 1974

Dear Dr. Nágera,

Thank you for your letter of February 18th. It is always nice to hear from you.

Yes, of course I'm quite ready to write a short introduction to your monograph [1]. I have a copy of it here so you don't have to send it.

England is not quite as bad as it sounds from the distance now and we are very happy that our winter so far did not last longer than 24 hours. Now our almond tree is in bloom already.

What you write about the unreasonableness of human beings is certainly true, I can subscribe to that.

Yours very sincerely,
Annafreud

1. She is referring here to the foreword she would write for Nágera's *Female Sexuality and the Oedipus Complex* (1975). New York: Jason Aronson, Inc.

DOCUMENT 127   ANNA FREUD

20 Maresfield Gardens
London

May 16, 1974

Dear Dr. Nágera,

The German translation of your Basic Psychoanalytic Concepts arrived a few moments ago and I am delighted to see the book and to have it. I do hope the translation has been done well. Thank you very much.

Yours sincerely
Annafreud

DOCUMENT 128   ANNA FREUD

20 Maresfield Gardens
London

August 20, 1974

Dear Dr. Nágera,

Thank you for your letter of July 31st. It was long delayed in the mail and only arrived just now.

I am sorry that I have been so slow with my Preface [1], but here it is at last. I hope that it is what you wanted. If you should wish for any changes, there may still be time to return it and let me know how to alter it.

Our last months here have not been good ones. The first tragic event was that Mrs. Burlingham's eldest daughter, Mabbie, died [2] when visiting us in London. I do not know whether you knew her. She was a specially lovely person and her death hit us very hard.

Almost at the same time, my only sister [3] was very ill with a heart block, and then in hospital to have a pacemaker fitted. That happened just now and we hope for good results.

As you see, it is a hard time.

With good wishes for yourself and your family,
yours sincerely
Annafreud

1. This was Anna Freud's foreword for Nágera's book *Female Sexuality and the Oedipus Complex* (1975). New York: Jason Aronson, Inc.
2. Mary "Mabbie" Tiffany Burlingham (1917–1974) was Dorothy Burlingham's oldest daughter. She had been in psychoanalysis with Anna Freud in her youth in the 1920s in Vienna. She was married in 1938, was living in the United States, and was sometimes in analysis with Marianne Kris. In the 1970s marital problems emerged, as did worries about not channeling her talents into a profession. In 1974 she was in despair and went to England to visit her mother and re-enter analysis with Anna Freud. In July, while Anna and Dorothy were busy closing down the Clinic for the summer holidays, Mabbie, in her room at 20 Maresfield Gardens, took an overdose of sleeping pills, fell unconscious, and died in the hospital some days later (Young-Bruehl, 1983, pp. 420–423; Burlingham, 1989, p. 310).
3. Anna Freud was referring here to her sister Mathilde Hollitscher (1887–1978). She was Anna Freud's only surviving sister but not her "only sister." Her other sister was Sophie Halberstadt (1893–1920), who died after the First World War as a result of the Spanish flu.

DOCUMENT 129   ANNA FREUD

Female Sexuality and the Oedipus Complex (1975) New York: Jason Aronson, Inc., by Humberto Nágera. Foreword by Miss Anna Freud.

Foreword

Dr. H. Nágera's book is a welcome reminder of the profitable years spent by him in and for the Hampstead Child-Therapy Clinic. As expressed by him in his own introductory chapter, it was especially his work with the Clinic's Diagnostic Profile and his Chairmanship of the organization's Clinical Concepts Group which roused his interest in the limitations which still place the analyst's knowledge of female development far behind that gained of their male peers.

In his approach to the problem of female sexuality, Dr. Nágera is, thus, in a far more favorable position than many analytic authors who have tackled this difficult subject before him. While those who are only analysts of adults have to be content with reconstructing the childhood events which are responsible for the deviations from normality in later life, Nágera, in his additional capacities as child analyst and diagnostician of children, is privileged to see the developmental processes themselves in action. To assess their beneficial or adverse effect for adult sexual behavior, he has at his disposal not only the analyst's familiar notions of fixation and regression, but also the concept of progressive forward moves on prescribed developmental lines.

From firsthand experience and child-analytical cases, Nágera constructs four of such lines for drive development itself and demonstrates the possibility to examine each of them separately as to its intactness or disturbance: change of object, of erotogenic zone, of sexual and of active-passive position. But, possibly more important and also more revolutionary than this, he proceeds to discuss the intimate interaction of these with three other influences which simultaneously shape the individuals sex life: the innate variations in the strength of the different components instincts; the rate of progress on the line of ego development; and the environmental circumstances and experiences which either favor or interfere with orderly developmental progress. With such a multitude of forces at work, he does not find it surprising that the deviations from a normal outcome are as numerous and as complex as they prove to be.

He reverts repeatedly to one particular factor in female sexual development to which he attributes outstanding significance, namely, the absence of a leading erotogenic zone during the little girl's positive Oedipus complex. Even after all the other agents in this situation are disentangled from each other, he confesses himself still faced with the question how an organ appropriate for the discharge of masculine-active excitation can be adapted to the same function regarding passive-feminine strivings. He thus sees and describes the girl's sexual life until and beyond puberty as one deprived of an executive organ, a void which needs to be filled on the psychological side by means of mechanisms and processes such as identification, desexualization, sublimation, etc.

While being guided through these developmental vicissitudes, readers can have every confidence in an author who acknowledges the presence of obscurities where our present state of knowledge renders them inevitable and who refuses to simplify matters which are, by nature, complex.

Anna Freud
London, 1974

DOCUMENT 130   ANNA FREUD

20 Maresfield Gardens
London

October 9, 1974

Dear Dr. Nágera,

I was very pleased to have your letter of October 4th, and to know that the Introduction has arrived and that you were pleased with it. All I can do now is to wish the book every success.

I was most interested to hear about your seminars on the Profile. As you know, no one takes it up here in London, apart from us here in the Clinic and that makes it all the more enjoyable to know that there is interest for it in the U.S.

We are all right here apart from the past tragic happenings and we are working hard to secure the future of the Clinic, if anything concerning the future can be called secure nowadays.

With best regards from me and all your friends in the Clinic,

Yours sincerely
Annafreud

DOCUMENT 131   ANNA FREUD

20 Maresfield Gardens
London

February 7, 1975

Dear Dr. Nágera,

Your letter of January 23rd was very welcome even if all the news you gave in it is not as happy as one would like it to be. I am sorry about the decision of Basic Books, but it does not seem impossible to me that if they withdraw their interest from the book that another publisher, for example Yale University press, might take over.

What you say about the students' and analytic teachers' attitude towards the Three Essays and other books by my father did not surprise me [1]. I myself have no longer any connection with the teaching functions in the Institute here, but from what Dr. Yorke tells me the difficulties are exactly the same. Neither students nor their teachers have any appreciation of past work anymore. They are going further and further away from it in the present. This seems to be the present trend and one feels it everywhere. You know how hard we try in the Clinic to create a completely different atmosphere, but even so I feel the danger sometimes.

I am very pleased that more and more of our graduates go to you and I do hope that you will find them useful. The only one about whom I have my doubts is Mrs. Temple [2]. I suppose you remember her from your time with us as not quite what was wanted. Of course it is a long time ago and she may have changed for the better. There is always this possibility.

At the moment we have an influx of 7 graduates from a medical college in Philadelphia who are supposed to stay with us for six months to get an impression of the work. The college pays for it and we are really not in a position to pass by such opportunities. We were rather afraid of undertaking the task, but it seems to be turning out much better than expected.

You have all my best wishes in these difficult times.

Yours sincerely,
Annafreud

1. Anna Freud was bemoaning the fact that psychoanalysts are getting further and further away from the original texts and basic principles (libido theory) of psychoanalysis. Nágera recalled: "She mentioned these people [that were moving away from the basic principles of psychoanalysis] on occasion, particularly Kohut, who was also a good friend of hers."
2. Pseudonym.

DOCUMENT 132   ANNA FREUD

20 Maresfield Gardens
London

July 25, 1975

Dear Dr. Nágera,

Your beautiful book [1] just arrived and I want to thank you very much for it. I am so glad that it has been published.

I missed you at the Congress [2], but I do not think that you missed very much. I am glad that the holidays are beginning now.

Yours sincerely,
Annafreud

1. *Female Sexuality and the Oedipus Complex* (1975). New York: Jason Aronson, Inc.
2. The 29th International Psychoanalytical Association Congress in London, England—Changes in Psychoanalytic Practice and Experience: Theoretical, Technical and Social Implications.

DOCUMENT 133   ANNA FREUD

20 Maresfield Gardens
London

October 8, 1975

Dear Dr. Nágera,

I was very pleased to have your letter of September 17th that followed me to Ireland, where I had a very pleasant holiday until October 1st when work began again.

As regards your book on the obsessional neuroses, you know I was always very interested in it, just as the obsessional neurosis was always my favorite subject for learning and teaching. I believe that there is no other mental disturbance better suited to display the interplay of forces in the mind. Therefore when the time comes I shall be glad to co-operate with a preface.

I have to confess that I am rather glad that Mrs. Temple [1] coming to you doesn't seem to work out. We never thought highly of her as a student and I think she would not have answered your requirements, certainly not for teaching others. It is quite a different matter with Marian Caplan and I am enclosing a recommendation for her on a separate sheet.

I did not know that you had also become president of the Institute. I feel sorry that you lost a good friend and colleague immediately. There are not so many around and the younger ones do not always replace them.

Life in England is not especially easy at the moment and I am glad for you that you have escaped the financial consequences here.

You did not miss anything by not coming to the Congress. The impressions were much more painful than pleasant.

Yours sincerely,
Annafreud

1. Pseudonym

DOCUMENT 134   ANNA FREUD

20 Maresfield Gardens
London

September 7, 1976

Dear Dr. Nágera,

Let me know whether this [1] will do or whether you want any corrections or amendments. I hope it comes in time.

Yours sincerely,
Annafreud

1. Anna Freud's foreword to Nágera's *Obsessional Neuroses: Developmental Psychopathology* (1976). New York: Jason Aronson, Inc.

DOCUMENT 135   ANNA FREUD

Obsessional Neuroses: Developmental Psychopathology (1976). New York: Jason Aronson, Inc. By Humberto Nágera. Foreword by Miss Anna Freud.

FOREWORD

The motivation for this elaborate and painstaking piece of work is revealed clearly in the quotation from Freud which initiates it [1]. Humberto Nágera shares Freud's belief that the obsessional neurosis is the most rewarding subject of analytic research, no other mental phenomena displaying with equal clarity the human quandary of relentless and unceasing battles between innate impulses and acquired moral demands.

In the main part of his book, the author traces Freud's insights into the subject as they advanced and broadened out from their first tentative beginnings in 1895 to some final pronouncements in 1939. He orders these formulations under meaningful headings which range from merely terminological and chronological concerns to the dynamic contributions made to the symptomatology by processes in id, ego and superego.

From this invaluable guide for study, which no average reader could provide for himself, he proceeds with similar thoroughness to the statements made by Freud's coworkers and immediate followers, giving preference among them to two notable teachers and chroniclers of psychoanalysis: Hermann Nunberg and Otto Fenichel. Nevertheless, in regard to these as well as to many of the other clinical and theoretical contributors, he deplores the scarcity of original findings and characterizes the main bulk of publications after Freud as merely amplifying and corroborating.

In his last chapters, Nágera enumerates the directions in which he feels the study of obsessional phenomena may yield further profit. He notes among these clearer distinctions (1) between transient obsessional symptoms as they arise during the ongoing conflicts of the anal-sadistic stage and the obsessional neurosis proper, caused by later regression to that level; (2) between the consequences of obsessionality for normal or abnormal character formation; (3) between obsessive characters on the one hand and the obsessive pathology on the other hand; and (4) between the harm done to a functioning personality by hysterical interferences and that done by obsessional interferences. Finally, and most important, he advocates a developmental approach to the etiological problems of the obsessional neurosis – that is, one in which not only a fixation point on the anal-sadistic level is considered of major importance, but one in which the contributions from all, earlier or later, developmental phases are given their due.

It is in this respect especially that the author's dealings with the problems of the obsessional neurosis constitute a welcome continuation of his earlier explorations of developmental disturbances and developmental conflicts as the possible forerunners of true neurotic conflicts, i.e., a continuation of his

efforts to create a developmental psychology which encompasses the normal and abnormal problems of all stages of human growth.
Anna Freud 1976

1. "Obsessional neurosis is unquestionably the most interesting and repaying subject of analytic research. But as a problem it has not yet been mastered." Sigmund Freud—*Inhibitions, Symptoms and Anxiety.*

DOCUMENT 136   ANNA FREUD

20 Maresfield Gardens
London

October 18, 1978

Dear Dr. Nágera,

Thank you very much for your letter of September 14th. In the meantime I also had news about you from Barrie Biven [1] who is just visiting here, and sounds very pleased with his life and work in Ann Arbor. I would be very pleased to know whether you are equally pleased with him and whether he does honor to his training with us [2]

I'm very curious how the Symposium [3] will turn out and I find insight a very intriguing subject. As you probably know, I have been asked to write a short introduction to it and I recorded this yesterday. But I had little of value to say beside stating the fact that children have no insight, which you know anyway. I read Hansi Kennedy's paper on the subject and I think it is very good indeed. I look forward to your impressions.

It is very nice about the Japanese and Portuguese translations of the Basic Concepts. It almost sounds as if people liked us all the better the further away they are. But I shall try with Yale Press, since people from there visit me next week anyway.

You ask about Bill Thompson [4]. I wonder what I should say. He means very well but I would not class him with our stronger successes.

I am glad that you have such good things to say about Danny [5]. Not all parents can be pleased like that with their teenagers.

Do let me know after the Symposium what you felt about it.

Yours sincerely,
Annafreud

1. Barrie Biven is a child analyst who trained at the Hampstead Clinic. Nágera later brought him to work at the University of Michigan's Children's Psychiatric Hospital.
2. Many of the letters reflect the confidence between Humberto Nágera and Anna Freud as they discuss various colleagues and Anna Freud expresses her pleasure or doubts about this one and that.
3. This was the Symposium on Insight that Nágera organized in Detroit, where Hansi Kennedy came as a representative from the Hampstead Clinic, and Miss Freud sent a taped recording in which she sounded weak and not well.
4. Pseudonym
5. Danny is one of Humberto and Gloria Nágera's children.

DOCUMENT 137   ANNA FREUD

20 Maresfield Gardens
London

December 20, 1978

Dear Dr. Nágera,

Your letter of December 8th only came two days ago. I don't know why it took such a long time.

In any case, it is not too late now to thank you and to say that we of the Hampstead Clinic are very grateful for whatever money has been collected, and as you well know from the past, we can do with any amount, small or large. It is also nice to look forward to a repetition of this event [1].

Hansi Kennedy told me a lot about the proceedings and of course I had read the two main papers. She also brought me your paper about the institutional arrangements necessary for children and I am very impressed by it. I think you are 100% right and one only wonders why such things have not been done long ago. I hope your paper will make a public impression and that it's advice will be followed.

Winter is never a very easy time and at the moment Mrs. Burlingham is in bed with some respiratory trouble [2] which is dragging on for quite a while now. Therefore we are quite uncertain still whether there will be a proper Christmas holiday, and whether we will be able to leave London.

With many greetings to you and Christmas and New Year wishes,
Yours sincerely,
Annafreud

1. The proceeds from the conference on Insight in Detroit went to the Hampstead Clinic in London.
2. Dorothy Burlingham spent a lifetime struggling with respiratory troubles and they were apparently resurging, but by 1978 she was also 87 years old and so these sorts of medical problems were taking on new implications.

DOCUMENT 138   ANNA FREUD

20 Maresfield Gardens
London

January 8, 1979

Dear Dr. Nágera,

Thank you very much for your letter of December 22nd.

I do look forward to your Comparison between Adults and Children as regards Insight [1]. I also had some further thoughts about it and I wonder whether as usual our thoughts meet.

The article hasn't come yet, but I look forward to it.

Yours sincerely,
Annafreud

1. "Insight in Children and Adults" was published in Nágera's *The Developmental Approach to Child Psychopathology* (1981). New York: Jason Aronson, Inc. pp. 129–151.

DOCUMENT 139   ANNA FREUD

20 Maresfield Gardens
London

December 14, 1979

Dear Dr. Nágera,

Thank you very much for your cable [1].
It all feels very sad and empty now.

Yours sincerely Annafreud

1. Dorothy Burlingham died on November 20, 1979. She was Anna Freud's closest friend and confidant for over fifty years. When Nágera heard the news of her death he sent a cable to Miss Freud with his condolences.

DOCUMENT 140   W. ERNEST FREUD

35 Basing Hill
London

March 3, 1980

Dear Humberto,

Just a line to say that I will be at the Child Psycho-Analysis Meeting in Cambridge, leaving here on March 27th. I will be staying [with] Anne [last name and address omitted] and we would very much like to invite you. She is the Van Gogh lady, in case you may not remember immediately.

After Boston to a conference in New Haven, April 11–13, and then for a few days to Cleveland before returning via Boston.

I very much hope to see you in Cambridge. Meanwhile with best wishes to you, Gloria and the family.

As ever,
Ernest [1]

1. W. Ernest Freud

DOCUMENT 141   ANNA FREUD

20 Maresfield Gardens
London

April 5, 1980

Dear Dr. Nágera,

I feel badly that it took me so long to answer your letter. The reason is not that it was not a good letter. On the contrary, it understood so much what I feel that it touched me very much. And, since I try very hard not to feel, or rather not to display feelings [1], it made me shut up instead of opening up.

Mrs. Burlingham and I often talked about it how it would be for the other when one of us died after a companionship of a little more than 50 years. We knew that it had to come since she by then was 88 and I am more than 84. But the expectation is never quite the same as the happening. I think that it was better this way with her dying first since the opposite would have been too hard for her.

One of the things my father taught me was not to "kick at fate". I try to follow that. Life is empty of pleasure, but there is work and that has to be enough at present.

I can fully understand what you say and feel about the way our colleagues (so many of them) tear bits out of psychoanalysis and destroy the center of it. I think as you do. I do not see how psychoanalysis can survive without the quantitative point of view. They call it the "energy concept" which is a misnomer in itself. If there is no libido theory, analysis seems to cease to work.

Also I am not surprised that you are disappointed in the University. From the very beginning, psychoanalysis and University never made a workable alliance, even if many attempts were made and many people thought it would work. It never did, from the first attempts under Alexander [2] in Chicago onwards. Only in Holland there were some successes.

I write to your University address since I do not have your private one; I never had. I think that I am lucky to have the Clinic which makes me independent of the other analytic organizations.

I shall send you my attempt at a paper on Insight which I wrote down only now. There are no copies until after the holiday.

With many greetings,
yours sincerely
Annafreud

1. Sigmund Freud was also known to be very discreet in the display of his emotions.
2. Franz Alexander, M.D. (1891–1964) was a Hungarian psychoanalyst who was mentored by Karl Abraham. When Freud's son, Oliver, developed an obsessional neurosis he was sent to Franz Alexander for psychoanalytic treatment. Alexander is considered one of the founders of psychosomatic medicine and coined the term "corrective emotional experience." In 1930 he immigrated to the United States and became Visiting Professor of Psychoanalysis at the University of Chicago.

20, MARESFIELD GARDENS
LONDON. NW3 5SX
01-435 2002

April 5, 1980.

Dear Dr. Nagera,

    I feel badly that it took me so long to answer your letter. The reason is not that it was not a good letter. On the contrary, it understood so much what I feel that it touched me very much. And, since I try very hard not to feel, or rather not to display feelings, it made me shut up instead of opening up.

    Mrs. Burlingham and I often talked about it how it would be for the other when one of us died after a companionship of a little more than 50 years. We knew that it had to come since she by then was 88 and I am more than 84. But the expectation is never quite the same as the happening. I think that it was better this way with her dying first since the opposite would have been too hard for her.

    One of the things my father taught me was not to "kick at fate". I try to follow that. Life is empty of pleasure, but there is work and that has to be enough at present.

    I can fully understand what you say and feel about the way our colleagues (so many of them) tear bits out of psychoanalysis and destroy the center of it. I think as you do. I do not see how psychoanalysis can survive without the quantitative point of view. They call it the "energy concept" which is a misnomer in itself. If there is no libido theory, analysis seems to cease to work.

    Also I am not surprised that you are disappointed in the University. From the very beginning, psychoanalysis and University never made a workable alliance, even if many attempts were made and many people thought it would work. It never did, from the first attempts under Alexander in Chicago onwards. Only in Holland there were some successes.

    I write to your University address since I do not have your private one; I never had. I think that I am lucky to have the Clinic which makes me independent of the other analytic organisations.

    I shall send you my attempt at a paper on Insight which I wrote down only now. There are no copies until after the holiday.

With many greetings,
        yours sincerely

                Anna Freud

DOCUMENT 142   ANNA FREUD

20 Maresfield Gardens
London

September 11, 1980

Dear Dr. Nágera,

May I ask you a favor please?

A leading pediatrician from England who has been a member of my pediatricians' group for very many years will visit Ann Arbor on 28th October for lecturing somewhere. It would be very nice if she could contact you and hear from you a bit about plans and developments in the analytic pediatricians' field in Ann Arbor in recent years.

Her name is Dr. Christine Cooper, and she is an unusually nice, clever and understanding woman who has done a great deal in her field for underprivileged children. It would be very nice if you would not mind seeing her.

Yours sincerely,
Annafreud

DOCUMENT 143   ANNA FREUD

20 Maresfield Gardens
London

July 28, 1981

Dear Dr. Nágera,

Many thanks for your nice letter of July 3rd.

Your question concerning my Mike Shervin [1] is not quite easy to answer. He worked quite hard in the Course, but he was certainly one of our weaker students. I do not know how he developed since he left us.

Many greetings, Yours sincerely, Annafreud

1. Pseudonym

DOCUMENT 144   W. ERNEST FREUD

35 Basing Hill
London

February 6, 1982

Dear Humberto,

Thank you for your letter of the 28th of January (postmark Feb. 2) which just arrived. As already mentioned over the phone, I shall be pleased to come to Monterey [1] on Friday, May 28 and Saturday, May 29th, to present a paper on "Range of the Ego Modalities in a Case of Overeating" (I quote the original title) and one on "Prenatal Attachment and Bonding." I am enclosing a copy of my C.V. With luck, I may even find the original diagnostic profile you did on Miss W. I will make a search for it after my return from the States. Or, you may still have a copy.

My travel agents are slow in providing the required information. I plan to arrive sometime on Thursday, 27th of May and return on Sunday, 30th. I will let you know when I get the details. It would be helpful for me to know whether I should get a ticket with a fixed (unchangeable) date or one with which the date(s) can be altered, if required. The latter is, I think, about £100 more expensive. I would appreciate it if you could phone me about this. I can then get the tickets before my departure from here for the States, i.e. before March 3rd.

In the meantime, I hope, my letter of January 28th reached you. It now looks as if visiting other parts of the States in connection with the Mexico trip would be rather expensive.

With best wishes to you, Gloria, and the children,
Ernest [2]

1. Monterey, Mexico
2. W. Ernest Freud

DOCUMENT 145   W. ERNEST FREUD

35 Basing Hill
London

May 10, 1982

Dear Humberto,

I have been back here for a few days and found the program of the May 28/29 conference in Monterey on my return, as well as a letter from Dra. Maria E. Rangel who would like to have a C.V., a photograph and a copy of the papers I am presenting. Am I correct in remembering that you have dealt with this? In any case the talk on "Prenatal Attachment and Bonding" has not been written up, and the one on The Range of Ego

Intake Modalities in a Case of Overeating I have always been reticent to circulate for reasons of confidentiality. I am not sure that there is a passable photo of me,—in fact, I suggested to the Topeka Society, for a similar purpose, to use the photo in Jones' biography of Freud ("Freud with his grandsons Ernst and Heinerle, Hamburg 1920"), in volume III, between pages 48 & 49, which is in any case more flattering than what can be seen nowadays.

I also just received a charming letter from my prospective guide, which raised all sorts of fantasies, hoping she will turn out to be as attractive as her letter. Shall I take it that you have advised them of the arrival of my flight from Houston?

[Short section omitted as distracting and irrelevant]

Miss Freud is in a poor state, having some difficulty with speech and her left hand and with swallowing. She cannot stand or walk, as her sense of balance is affected. It looks as if progress will be slow. [1]

I am very much looking forward to seeing you in Mexico. In the meantime my very best regards, also to Gloria and the children.

Yours,
Ernest

P.S. On my travels I met in Columbia, Missouri Prof. Armando R. Favazza, who told me he trained with you and who sends greetings.

1. On March 1, 1982 Anna Freud suffered a stroke.

DOCUMENT 146   W. ERNEST FREUD

20 Maresfield Gardens
London

August 23, 1982

Dear Humberto,

Thank you for your kind inquiry of August 12th and also for the copy of your Monterey paper.

My sincere apologies for not writing earlier, but I have been under rather a lot of personal strain, arising out of my domestic situation. I won't bother you with all the details.

[Short section omitted as distracting and irrelevant]

I am living in digs but am using the Maresfield Gardens address.

[Short section omitted as distracting and irrelevant]

On Saturday I am off to Cologne for my yearly two weeks' stint of brief classical analyses with the staff of one of the psychological institutes of the university there. It will be a welcome diversion. However, from past experience I know that it will be all analysis and nothing else, i.e. lack of social life distractions. In general, I will have to rebuild any social life here, and I am on the look out for attractive younger females. Please let me know if any of your acquaintances pass through London.

As to Mexico, I remain indebted to you for inviting me to Monterey. I have thanked them for their fabulous hospitality which was really quite out of this world, and it was in many ways a godsend for me. Mexico City paled by comparison, though it was interesting and rewarding. My impression was that the group there has some difficulties and as a visitor I could fortunately steer clear of them. I am naturally very sorry that Mexico's financial situation has deteriorated so much. During my stay I had already been told as much and people had been concerned about it. I can only hope that it won't put an end to the very pleasurable professional visits of yours, and in many respects the Spanish-speaking environment must be like a second home for you quite apart from the charming personal contacts you have built.

Anna Freud has been home for some months now, but her condition has not basically improved. It is a pathetic household now also with Paula (the househelp) getting more senile. Anna's disturbing feature is a speech disturbance, so that I find it difficult to communicate with her. Mentally, she is still very lucid when she is not tired. Her condition varies in terms of being rested or fatigued, and she easily tires these days. She can't walk and is either in bed or on a sunbed on the garden veranda or in a wheelchair. She is very dependent on the people looking after her (she has a day- and a night-nurse, mainly to help with going to the toilet), and it must be heartbreaking for such an active person. However, so far she seems to have been taking it well. It is, of course, anybody's guess how much longer this will go on. So that has been hanging over my head too.

It has been good sharing this with you. Please let me know if you plan to visit London. There are still a number of good years in me if my health stands up to it all, and I hope to make the best of it. If I get half a chance I will move to Australia hoping to make a better living there. I know, it sounds a bit fantastic at my age, but why not?!

Do write again! I am always pleased to hear from a good friend. Meanwhile, with best wishes to you, Gloria and the family,

As always,
Ernest

DOCUMENT 147   W. ERNEST FREUD

20 Maresfield Gardens
London

October 26, 1982

Dear Humberto,

Thank you for your kind and thoughtful letter of October 18th.

Yes, it seems that Anna Freud passed away peacefully,—I had a word with her doctor the other day, who also said that she did not die from anything in particular, but that there just wasn't any more energy left; she had practically slept all the time for the last few days before it happened. [1]

It is, of course, a big change for me. Somewhat unexpectedly, I reacted with a sense of relief, because she had presented for me a terrific—and often crippling—superego. I wonder to what extent similar aspects might influence the clinic, which seems to count on continuing more or less as before. I would think that the only real threat to the clinic would be if they ever ran out of funds. But perhaps there are enough well-intentioned rich people about to prevent this.

You may have heard that Paula has gone back to Austria, to stay in a very good Old Peoples' Home there. It was a big decision, and several people thought hard about it before giving her the choice. A seemingly dedicated nephew and his wife are looking after her.

You are right in saying that psychoanalysis is now an orphan. I hope the orphan will successfully survive!

Let me know how things will develop with you.

With kind regards and best wishes, also to Gloria and the children,
Yours,
Ernest

1. Anna Freud died on October 9, 1982.

It is fitting that we close this collection with two letters; the first, from a 14 year-old boy asking Anna Freud what she considers to be the "essential personal qualities in a future psychoanalyst"; the second, Anna Freud's reply. Nágera knew the boy's parents, and that is how he ended up with the letters. Anna Freud's letter was previously published by Heinz Kohut in his 1968 article, "The Evaluation of Applicants for Psychoanalytic Training," in the International Journal of Psychoanalysis, Volume 49, pp. 548–554.

We are all familiar with Sigmund Freud's vision of the ideal psychoanalytic institute in which candidates would study depth psychology, biology, the sexual life, psychiatric symptomatology, as well as "the history of civilization, mythology, the psychology of religion and the science of literature." (S. Freud, 1926/1959a, SE 20, p. 228) In 1966 Anna Freud wrote on this topic as well in "The Ideal Psychoanalytic Institute: A Utopia" (A. Freud, 1966/1971, Vol. XII, pp. 73–93). But in the following, thanks to a fourteen-year-old boy, we learn what Anna Freud considered the essential personal qualities of a psychoanalyst.

DOCUMENT 148   JOHN

Ann Arbor, Michigan

February 14, 1961

Dear Miss Freud:

I'm a fourteen-year-old boy. I would like to make psychoanalysis my life work. My father is a psychoanalyst and this inspiration is not the only one which has led me to choose this field. I am now required, as a ninth grade student at Tappan Junior High School, to write a paper on the vocation of my choice.

I would be most grateful for any suggestions that you might have. What would you consider essential personal qualities in a future psychoanalyst? What suggestions as to preparation would you have beyond requirements listed in the catalogues of psychoanalytic institutes?

Any suggestions that would help me to do my best in becoming a psychoanalyst will be very deeply appreciated.

Respectfully yours,
John

DOCUMENT 149   ANNA FREUD

20 Maresfield Gardens
London

February 22, 1961

Dear John,

I was very interested in your letter of February 14th and I shall like to help you, if I can.

You ask me what I consider essential personal qualities in a future psychoanalyst. The answer is comparatively simple. If you want to be a real psychoanalyst you have to have a great love of the truth, scientific truth as well as personal truth, and you have to place this appreciation of truth higher than any discomfort at meeting unpleasant facts, whether they belong to the world outside or to your own inner person.

Further, I think that a psychoanalyst should have very wide interests, which means beyond the limits of the medical field. He should be interested in facts that belong to sociology, religion, literature, history and culture in general. If he does not achieve that, his outlook on the people, who will be his patients, will remain too narrow.

This former point contains at the same time the necessary preparations beyond the requirements made on candidates of psychoanalysis in the institutes. You ought to be a great reader and become acquainted with the literature of many countries and cultures. In the great literary figures you will find people who know at least as much of human nature, as the psychiatrists and psychologists try to do.

Does that answer your question?

Yours sincerely,
Annafreud

REFERENCES

Abraham, H. C., & Freud, E. L. (Eds.). (1965). *The letters of Sigmund Freud and Karl Abraham, 1907–1926.* New York: Basic Books.

Bateson, J. (2010). *The holocaust survivors at Weir Courtney, Lingfield.* The RH7 History Group. http://www.rh7.org/factshts/holocst.pdf (accessed September 13, 2013).

Benveniste, D. (2015). *The interwoven lives of Sigmund, Anna and W. Ernest Freud: Three generations of psychoanalysis.* New York: International Psychoanalytic Books.

Blanck, G. & Blanck, R. (1974). *Ego psychology: Theory and practice.* New York: Colombia University Press.

Boehlich. W. & Pomerans, A.J. (Eds. and Trans.) (1990). *The Letters of Sigmund Freud to Eduard Silberstein 1871–1881.* Cambridge, Mass.: Belknap Press of Harvard University Press.

Brinich, P. (1981). Application of the Metapsychological Profile to the assessment of deaf children. *Psychoanalytic Study of the Child.* 36: 3–32.

Burlingham, D. (1975). Special problems of blind infants: Blind Baby Profile. *Psychoanalytic Study of the Child.* 30: 3–13.

Burlingham, M. J. (1989). *The last Tiffany: A biography of Dorothy Tiffany Burlingham.* New York: Atheneum.

Busch, F. (1974). Dimensions of the first transitional object. *Psychoanalytic Study of the Child,* 29:215–229.

Busch, F. & McKnight, J. (1973). Parental attitudes and the development of the primary transitional object. *Child Psychiatry and Human Development,* Vol. 4(1), Fall 1973.

Busch, F., Nágera, H., & Pezzarossi, G. (1973). Primary transitional objects. *Journal of the American Academy of Child Psychiatry,* 1973 Apr; 12 (2):193–214.

Fonagy, P. (2001). Joseph Sandler (1927–1998). *International Journal of Psychoanalysis,* 82:815–817.

Greenson, R. (1967). *The Technique and Practice of Psychoanalysis.* New York: International Universities Press.

Freud, A. (1936/1966). *The ego and the mechanisms of defense. The writings of Anna Freud,* Vol. II. New York: International Universities Press.

——— (1951/1968). An experiment in group upbringing. In A. Freud, *The Writings of Anna Freud,* Vol. IV, 163–229.

——— (1962). Assessment of childhood disturbances. *Psychoanalytic Study of the Child.* 17:149–158, And in *The Writings of Anna Freud,* Vol. V, pp. 26–59.

——— (1965). *Normality and pathology in childhood: Assessments of development. The Writings of Anna Freud,* Vol. VI, pp. 3–24. New York: International Universities Press.

——— (1966/1971). The ideal psychoanalytic institute: A utopia. *The Writings of Anna Freud,* Vol. XII, pp. 73–93).

——— (1970/1971). The symptomatology of childhood: An attempt at classification. *Psychoanalytic Study of the Child.* 25:19–41, 1970. And in *Problems of Psychoanalytic Training, Diagnosis, and the Technique of Therapy 1966–1970. The Writings of Anna Freud Volume VII.* New York: International Universities Press (1971) pp. 157–188.

——— (1988). The nursery school of the Hampstead Child-Therapy Clinic. *Bulletin of the Anna Freud Centre.* Vol. 11, Part 4.

——— (2005). *Normalidad y patología en la niñez : evaluación del desarrollo.* (H. Nágera, Trans.). Buenos Aires: Paidos.

Freud, A., Nágera, H. and Freud, (W.E. (1965). Metapsychological assessment of the adult personality: The adult profile. *Psychoanalytic Study of the Child.* 20: 9–41. And in *Writings of Anna Freud,* Vol. 5, 60–75.

Freud, A., Nágera, H. and Bolland, J. *Anna Freud's Developmental Profile: Modifications and present form.* Carter-Jenkins Center website.

Freud, I. (1990). *Unpublished memoirs of Irene Freud.* (March 12, 1990). W. Ernest Freud Archive. Die Bundesarchiv, Koblenz, Germany.

Freud, S. (1905/1953). Three essays toward a theory of sexuality. In J. Strachey (Ed. & Trans.) *The standard edition of the complete psychological works of Sigmund Freud* (Vol. VII) London: Hogarth Press.

——— (1909/1955). Two case histories: "Little Hans" and "The "Rat Man." In James Strachey (Ed. & Trans.), *Standard Edition.* Vol. X. London: Hogarth Press.

——— (1920/1955). Beyond the pleasure principle. In James Strachey (Ed. & Trans). *Standard Edition,* Vol. XVIII, 7–64. London: Hogarth Press.

——— (1923, 1961). The ego and the id. In J. Strachey (Ed. & Trans.) *The Standard Edition* Vol. XIX, pp. 12–66. London: Hogarth Press.

――― (1926/1959a). The question of lay analysis. In James Strachey (Ed. & Trans.). *Standard Edition,* Vol. XX, 183–258. London: Hogarth Press.

――― (1932–1936/1964*). New introductory lectures on psycho-analysis and other works.* In James Strachey (Ed. & Trans.), *Standard Edition.* Vol. XXII. London: Hogarth Press.

――― (1933/1964b). New introductory lectures on psycho-analysis. In James Strachey (Ed. & Trans.), *Standard Edition,* Vol. XXII:7–182. London: Hogarth Press.

Freud, W. E. (1967). Assessment of early infancy: Problems and considerations. (Also known as The Baby Profile—Part I). *Psychoanalytic Study of the Child,* 22:216–238.

Freud, W.E. (1971). The Baby Profile—Part II. *Psychoanalytic Study of the Child,* 26:172–194.

Friedmann, M. (1988). The Hampstead Clinic Nursery: The first 20 years (1957–1978). *Bulletin of the Anna Freud Centre,* 11:277–287.

Furman, E. (1974). *A child's parent dies: Studies in childhood bereavement.* New Haven and London: Yale University Press.

Furman, E. (1992). *Toddlers and their mothers: A study in early personality development.* Madison, CT: International Universities Press.

Heller, P. (1992). *Anna Freud's letters to Eva Rosenfeld.* Madison, CT: International Universities Press.

Hoffer, W. (1955). *Psychoanalysis: Practical and research aspects.* Baltimore: The Williams and Wilkins Co.

REFERENCES

Holder, A. (2005). *Anna Freud, Melanie Klein, and the psychoanalysis of children and adolescents*. London: Karnac Books.

Kennedy, H. (1978). The Hampstead Centre for the Psychoanalytic Study and Treatment of Children. *Bulletin of the Hampstead Clinic*. (1978)1. pp. 119–120.

King, P. & Steiner, R. (1991). *The Freud-Klein controversies, 1941–45*. London: Tavistock.

Klein, M. (1932). *The psycho-analysis of children*. London: Hogarth Press.

Laufer, M. (1965) Assessment of adolescent disturbances: The Application of Anna Freud's Diagnostic Profile. *Psychoanalytic Study of the Child*. 20: 99–123.

Meyer-Palmedo, I. (Ed.) (2013). *Sigmund Freud Anna Freud: Correspondence 1904–1938*. (N. Somers, Trans.). Hoboken, NJ: Wiley & Sons.

Molnar, M. (1992). *The diary of Sigmund Freud, 1929–1939: A record of the final decade*. London: Freud Museum Publications.

Moran, G. (1988). Editorial note. *Bulletin of the Anna Freud Centre*, 11, 263.

Nágera, H. (1966). *Early childhood disturbances, the infantile neurosis, and the adulthood disturbances: Problems of a developmental psychoanalytic psychology*. As Monograph No. 2 (1966) in *The Monograph Series of The Psychoanalytic Study of the Child*.

——— (1967). *Vincent van Gogh: A Psychological Study*. New York: International Universities Press.

——— (1975). *Female sexuality and the oedipus complex*. New York: Jason Aronson, Inc.

——— (1976). *Obsessional neuroses: developmental psychopathology.* New York: Jason Aronson, Inc.

——— (1981). *The developmental approach to child psychopathology.* New York: Jason Aronson., Inc.

Nágera, H. et al. (1969). *Volume I: Basic psychoanalytic concepts on the libido theory.* London: George Allen and Unwin Ltd.

——— (1969). *Volume II: Basic psychoanalytic concepts on the theory of dreams.* New York: Basic Books, Inc.

——— (1970). *Volume III: Basic Psychoanalytic Concepts on the Theory of Instincts.* London: George Allen and Unwin Ltd.

——— (1970). *Volume IV: Basic psychoanalytic concepts on metapsychology, conflicts, anxiety and other subjects.* New York: Basic Books, Inc.

Rangell, L. (2004) *My life in theory.* New York: Other Press.

Sandler, J. (1965). The Hampstead Child-Therapy Clinic. In *Aspects of family mental health in Europe,* 109–123. Geneva: World Health Organization,

Sandler, J. & Freud, A. (1985). *The analysis of defense: The ego and the mechanisms of defense revisited.* New York: International Universities Press.

Steiner, R. (2000). *"It is a new kind of diaspora": Explorations in the sociopolitical and cultural context of psychoanalysis.* London: Karnac Books.

Sterba, R. (1982). *Reminiscences of a Viennese psychoanalyst.* Detroit: Wayne State University Press.

Young-Bruehl, E. (1988). *Anna Freud: A biography.* New York: Summit Books.

Daniel Benveniste, PhD, is also the author of *The interwoven lives of Sigmund, Anna and W. Ernest Freud: Three generations of psychoanalysis* (2015). He is a clinical psychologist with a private practice in Bellevue, Washington. Originally from California, he did his training and began his practice and teaching in the San Francisco Bay Area. He lived and worked in Caracas, Venezuela from 1999 to 2010 and then relocated to the Pacific Northwest with his wife and colleague, Adriana Prengler de Benveniste.

Humberto Nágera, M.D. is a psychoanalyst and the Director of the Carter-Jenkins Center in Tampa, Florida. He did his psychiatric training in Havana, Cuba and his psychoanalytic training at the Institute of the British Psycho-Analytical Society while working concurrently at the Hampstead Clinic as a trusted colleague of Miss Anna Freud. He is the author of *Early childhood disturbances, the infantile neurosis, and the adulthood disturbances: Problems of a developmental psychoanalytic psychology* (1966); *Vincent van Gogh: A psychological study* (1967); *Female sexuality and the Oedipus complex* (1975); *Obsessional neuroses: Developmental psychopathology* (1976); *The developmental approach to child psychopathology* (1981); and is the lead co-author of the four volume Basic Psychoanalytic Concepts series addressing *Libido theory (1969), Theory of dreams (1969), Theory of instincts (1970),* and *Metapsychology, conflicts, anxiety and other subjects (1970).*

INDEX

Abraham, Karl, 6, 7, 126, 207, 219
Aichhorn, August, 3, 22, 179
Antiquity, 93, 94

Baker, Sheila, 64, 115, 167
Balkanyi, Charlotte, 106
Bene, Aggie, 114
Benveniste, Daniel, 1, 2, 219, 225
Bernays, Minna, 22
Bernfeld, Siegfried, 3, 7, 9, 22
Bibring, Grete, 188
Biven, Barrie, 201, 202
Blind children, 16, 17, 39, 42, 59, 60–62, 72, 79, 80, 86, 87, 155, 157, 219
Bolland, John, XII, 40, 41, 43, 69, 80, 99, 100, 113, 147, 221
Bonaparte, Marie, 3, 4
Bonnard, Augusta 14
Bose, G., 87
Bose, K., 86, 87
Bose, R., 86, 87
Brand, Jeanne, 89, 133, 134, 136
Brinich, Paul, 39, 219

British Psycho-Analytical Society, XI, 2, 11, 13, 15, 88, 173, 174, 177, 178, 225
Bry, Ava, 189, 190
Burgner, Mrs., 64
Burlingham, Dorothy, 3, 5, 7–9, 22, 26, 33, 39, 59, 60, 61, 86, 90, 156, 157, 167, 189, 192, 203, 205, 206, 219
Burlingham, Mary "Mabbie" Tiffany, 60, 192
Busch, Fred, 184, 185, 219, 220

Carter-Jenkins Center, XIII, 18, 40, 107, 221, 225
Casuso, Gabriel, XI
Colonna, Alice, 64, 115
Concept Groups (Core Psychoanalytic Concepts—Clinical and Theoretical), 3, 12, 15, 17, 35–38, 47, 49, 52, 58, 63–67, 70, 83, 115, 125, 140, 155, 157, 161–165, 168–172, 178, 180, 191, 193, 201, 224, 225
Cooper, Christine, 209

Crown, Dr., 101
Cuba, XI, XII, 1, 15, 18, 25, 178, 225

Dann, Gertrude, 13, 14
Dann, Sophie, 13, 14
Dansky, Eleanor, 64, 115
Day care, 8, 182, 183, 184
Demming, Julia, 9
Developmental Lines, 5, 15, 16, 41, 43, 51, 54, 55, 79, 80, 193
Developmental Profiles, 3, 5, 16, 17, 26, 31, 32, 38–44, 56, 57, 59, 60, 65, 71–73, 79, 80, 81–83, 87, 89–92, 99, 101, 102, 104–106, 117, 119, 120, 131–133, 135, 139, 146, 149, 155, 174, 178, 181, 193, 195, 210, 219, 221– 223
Dyer, Raymond, 2, 55

Edgcumbe, Rose, 2, 64, 115, 117
Eissler, Kurt, 27, 28, 46, 50, 85
Eissler, Ruth, 46, 87, 89, 96, 104

Fichtl, Paula, 22, 214, 215
Federn, Paul, 9
Fenichel, Otto, 49, 52, 200
Ferenczi, Sandor, 7, 59
First, Elsa, 115
Fleiss, Wilhelm, 37, 38
Frankl, Liselotte, 14, 32, 100, 116, 150
Freeman, Tom, 133

Freud, Anna, 1–19
   Anna Freud's Developmental Profile, 40–44
   Foreword to Nágera's book on Early Childhood Disturbances 121–122
   Foreword to Nágera's book on Vincent van Gogh 153
   Foreword to Nágera's books on Basic Psychoanalytic Concepts 163–166
   Foreword to Nágera's book on Female Sexuality 193–195
   Foreword to Nágera's book on Obsessional Neurosis 199–201
   Normality and Pathology in Childhood, 17, 40, 51, 54-56, 91, 107, 118, 167, 220
   Obsessional neurosis discussion IPA Congress 1965, 106–112
   Personality, XI–XIV, 23
   Reports, 63–70, 71–74, 78–80, 145–150
Freud, Colin, 88, 180
Freud, Ernst L., 147, 174, 175
Freud, Irene, 33, 88, 175, 176, 177, 180
Freud, Martha, 4, 5, 22, 175
Freud, Sigmund, 3. 9,13–15, 22, 28, 32, 35–38, 48, 60, 84, 87, 88, 94, 96, 106, 118, 123, 145, 159, 165, 177, 180, 185, 201, 207, 216, 219, 221, 223

INDEX

Sigmund Freud's advice, 116, 206
Freud, Sophie (Halberstadt), 4, 5, 6, 88, 192
Freud, W. Ernest, 2, 19, 33, 39, 57, 88, 89, 149, 157, 158, 174–178, 180, 205, 210, 211, 212–215, 219, 221, 225
Friedmann, Manna, 26, 179, 186
Frijling-Schreuder, Prof., 99, 100
Furman, Erna, 40, 132, 222
Furman, Robert, 131, 132

Gardiner, Muriel, 30, 33, 34
Gavshon, Audrey, 64, 115, 143
Gillespie, William H., 115
Glover, Edward, 10
Goldberger, Alice, 13, 62, 63
Goldstein, Joseph, 18
Goldstein, Sonja, 18
Greenacre, Phyllis, 115
Greenson, Ralph R., 49, 115, 220

Hacker, Prof., 185
Hartmann, Heinz, 32, 47, 48, 109, 110, 115, 144
Heimann, Paula, 122, 123
Heller, Peter, 7, 222
Hellman, Ilse, XI, 23, 24, 80, 135, 149, 174
Hodgson, Miss, 64
Hoffer, Hedwig, 29
Hoffer, Willi, 3, 9, 14, 21, 22, 25, 26, 29, 144, 186, 222

Holder, Alex, 12, 34, 35, 64, 80, 105, 115, 148, 223
Hug-Hellmuth, Hermine, 6

Index (Psychoanalytic)—see Psychoanalytic Index

Jackson (Edith) Nursery, 9, 26, 61, 177
Jones, Ernest, 3, 9, 22, 212
Jones, Galdys, 64, 115

Kawenoka, Maria, 115
Kearney, Lotte, 115
Kennedy, Hansi, 14, 17, 120, 174, 176, 188, 201–203, 223
Klein, Melanie, 3, 5–16, 22, 35, 116, 122–124, 144, 223
Koch, Ehud, 115
Kohut, Heinz, 4, 169, 196, 215
Kris, Ernst, 33, 48, 176
Kris, Marianne, 31, 192

Laufer, Moses, 39, 43, 64, 105, 106, 115, 139, 223
Leek, Peter, 160
Legg, Cecily, 115, 181
Letter opener, 158–160
Lorand, Sandor, 58, 59, 115
Lustman, Seymour, 174, 176

McDivitt, John B., 154
McKnight, Judith, 185, 220

Meers, Dale, 64, 80, 103, 115, 117
Meyer-Palmedo, Ingeborg, 2, 223
Myerson, Paul, 106
Michaels, Joseph J., 81–83, 85, 106, 107
Michigan, University of, XII, 18, 175, 181, 183, 184, 202, 206, 207
Morrison, Miss, 170

N.I.M.H. (National Institute of Mental Health), 27, 28, 41, 51, 65, 68, 71, 79, 133, 134, 145, 146, 151
Nágera, Danny, 202
Nágera, Mrs. Gloria, 26, 93, 125, 175, 177, 202, 205, 211, 212, 214, 215
Nágera, Humberto,
    Background, 1, 2, 15, 18
    Concept Groups—see Concept groups
    Day care—see Day care
    Foreword, XI–XIV
    Hampstead Clinic, 74–77
    Metapsychological Assessment of the Adult Personality, 39, 43, 57, 90, 178, 221
    Obsessional neurosis—see Obsessional neurosis
Nágera, Lisette, 185
Neurath, Lily, 37, 38, 64, 115
Nunberg, Hermann, 22, 141, 145, 200

Obsessional neurosis, 19, 53–55, 82, 100, 101, 106–112, 115, 118, 198–201, 224, 225

Oken, Donald, 145

Pollock, George H., 91, 102
Psychoanalytic Index, 17, 25–27, 35, 65, 66, 69, 79, 80, 146, 147, 149
Putzel, Renate, 32, 64, 120

Radford, Pat, 43, 64, 115
Rangel, Maria, E., 211
Rangell, Leo, 169, 182, 224
Rees, Katherine, 64, 115
Richardson, George A., 154, 156
Roiphe, Herman, 154
Rosenfeld, Eva, 3, 7, 60, 222
Ross, Helen, 51

Salome, Lou Andreas, 3, 4
Sandler, Joseph, 14, 16, 17, 27, 34, 35, 80, 147, 148, 150, 188, 220, 224
Sapir, Philip, 71, 78, 79, 134, 170
Schur, Max, 106, 111, 177
Silberstein, Eduard, 118, 219
Sklar, Mr., 33, 34
Solms, Dozent, 185
Solnit, Albert J., 18
Strachey, James, 10, 37, 38, 87, 95, 96, 98, 221, 222
Starks, Dr., 181
Sterba, Richard F., 83, 84, 115, 224
Stross, Josephine, 3, 9, 14, 175, 177

Tartakoff, Helen, 129
Thurtle, Kate, 134, 142, 174

INDEX

Unwin, Philip, 161–163, 224

Valenstein, Arthur, 106, 109, 110
Van Gogh, Vincent, 129, 130, 139, 140, 152, 153, 205, 223, 225

Waelder, Robert, 141
Waelder-Hall, Jenny, 26
Waggoner, Ray, 175

Wealer, Dr., 99
Weiss, Jula, 69, 143
Weissman, Philip, 106
Weitzner, Mrs., 64, 148
Windholz, Emanuel, 52, 53

Yorke, Clifford, 120, 157, 195
Young-Bruehl, Elizabeth, 2, 5–7, 32, 190, 192, 224

www.ingramcontent.com/pod-product-compliance
Lightning Source LLC
Chambersburg PA
CBHW050441240426
43661CB00055B/2464